A Day in Hollywood, A Night in the Ukraine

A musical

Book and lyrics by Dick Vosburgh

Music by Frank Lazarus

Samuel French — London
New York - Toronto - Hollywood

The musical material consists of Piano I and Piano II; there is a Piano III, which is used on stage. In addition, Samuel French Ltd can supply a tape consisting of Harp Music and Horses Hooves. Please enquire for details.

NOTE: A NIGHT IN THE UKRAINE may be performed on its own as a one-act musical. A separate one-act version of the score is available. Please enquire from Samuel French Ltd.

Important Credit and Billing Requirement

All producers must give credit to the authors in all programmes, advertising or publicizing of this work. The names of the authors must also appear on a separate line in which no other names appear, following the title of the work and printed in a size of type not less than fifty per cent (50 %) the size of the title type. Billing shall be in the following form:

(Name of Producer)

presents

A DAY IN HOLLYWOOD, A NIGHT IN THE UKRAINE

A MUSICAL

Book and Lyrics by
DICK VOSBURGH

Music by
FRANK LAZARUS

In addition, the following credits must appear in all programmes for this musical:

"EASY TO LOVE" by Cole Porter. Used with permission of Robert H. Montgomery, Jr. Trustee, The Cole Porter Musical and Literary Property Trusts.

"OVER THE RAINBOW" Words by E. Y. Harburg and Music by Harold Arlen. Used by permission of Robbins Music Corp.

"SLEEPY TIME GAL" Words by Joseph R. Alden and Raymond B. Egan, Music by Ange Lorenzo and Richard A. Whiting. Used by permission of Robbins Music Corp.

"AIN'T WE GOT FUN" Music by Richard A. Whiting and Lyrics by Gus Kahn and Raymond Egan. Used by permission of Gilbert Keye's Music/Warner Bros. Music.

"ON THE GOOD SHIP LOLLIPOP" by Sidney Clare and Richard A. Whiting. Used by permission of Sam Fox Publishing Co. Inc.

"TOO MARVELOUS FOR WORDS" by Johnny Mercer and Richard A. Whiting. Used by permission of Warner Bros. Music.

"JAPANESE SANDMAN" by Raymond Egan and Richard A. Whiting. Used by permission of Warner Bros. Music.

"HOORAY FOR HOLLYWOOD" by Johnny Mercer and Richard A. Whiting. Used by permission of Warner Bros. Music.

"LOUISE" by Leo Robin and Richard A. Whiting. Used by permission of Famous Music Corporation.

"BEYOND THE BLUE HORIZON" by Franke W. Harling, Leo Robin and Richard A. Whiting. Used by permission of Famous Music Corporation.

"THANKS FOR THE MEMORY" by Leo Robin and Ralph Rainger. Used by permission of Famous Music Corporation.

"TWO SLEEPY PEOPLE" by Hoagy Carmichael and Frank Loesser. Used by permission of Famous Music Corporation.

"DOUBLE TROUBLE" by Richard A. Whiting, Leo Robin and Ralph Rainger. Used by permission of Famous Music Corporation.

"COCKTAILS FOR TWO" by Sam Coslow and Arthur Johnston. Used by permission of Famous Music Corporation.

A DAY IN HOLLYWOOD
A NIGHT IN THE UKRAINE

In London, first performed at the New End Theatre in February 1979. The company played themselves in *A Day in Hollywood*, and in *A Night in the Ukraine* appeared as follows:

Mrs Pavlenko	Paddie O'Neil
Carlo	Frank Lazarus
Gino	Sheila Steafel
Serge B Samovar	John Bay
Nina	Maureen Scott
Constantine	Jon Glover
Masha	Pera Koston

The show transferred to The Mayfair Threatre in April 1979, with the same cast, except that the part of Masha was played by Alexandra Sebastian.

MUSICAL NUMBERS

DAY IN HOLLYWOOD

ACT I

A NIGHT IN THE UKRAINE

ACT II

CHARACTERS

ACT I: A Day in Hollywood
A musical revue

The Company (see the Production Notes)

The action of Act I takes place in the lobby of Grauman's Chinese Theatre

ACT II: A Night in the Ukraine
Loosely based on Chekhov's The Bear

Mrs Pavlenko, a rich widow
Carlo, Mrs Pavlenko's Italian footman
Gino, Mrs Pavlenko's gardener
Serge B Samovar, a Moscow Lawyer
Nina, Mrs Pavlenko's daughter
Constantine, a coachman
Masha, the maid
Sascha, a manservant

The action of Act II takes place in the morning room of the Pavlenko residence in the Ukraine before the Revolution

PRODUCTION NOTES

Set Design

Act I—A Day in Hollywood

In the Broadway production, 6 doors, capable of revolving, formed the back wall of the set. They suggested the doors that led from the lobby of Grauman's Chinese Theatre into the cinema auditorium. The doors were red on one side and black on the other, which made several visual combinations possible. (For convenience, the doors are numbered in the text from 1 to 6, reading from R to L.) In each door was a porthole in which the translucent glass (useful as an effect occasionally when lit from behind) could be lowered or raised, to enable performers to appear behind them, the open portholes framing their faces or, on occasion, their hands.

Above the doors was a platform running the full width from door 1 to door 6, concealed by a traveller which was opened when needed. This platform was actually a strip of stage, something like an oversized mail-slot, which revealed only the legs of the performers from the thighs down. We referred to it by the somewhat misleading title of "The Ankle-stage". Directly above it, and running its full length (out of sight of the audience, of course) was a bar, which was used by people on the Ankle-stage to steady themselves where necessary, and also—sparingly—for the airborne effect created when the dancers gripped it with both hands and raised their legs off the floor. The floor of the Ankle-stage was designed to look like the paving stones, with signed footprints, as they appear in the forecourt of Grauman's Chinese Theatre, but it was only visible to the audience when reflected in a tilted mirror, backing the Ankle-stage during the number "Famous Feet".

The Ankle-stage certainly enhanced the production, but repertory and amateur companies should note that Act I can conceivably be performed without the Ankle-stage and should explore other resourceful avenues if necessary.

The floor on the main stage was a shiny black, as were (1) the curved bar counter, UR, just in front and to the right of door 1, (2) the two benches (each a long, four-legged stool like a piano bench or a coffee table) placed DL and DR just within each proscenium wall, at right angles to the auditorium, and (3) the grand piano with a round, swivel stool, placed L, below and to the left of door 6.

Act II—A Night in the Ukraine

We are in pre-Revolutionary Russia, in Mrs Pavlenko's opulent villa. The style is Hollywood-Ukrainian. There are three entrances—UL, UR, and UC. (In the London production there were only two entrances, L and R.) The grand piano is L, with its round swivel stool. RC is a padded black leather *chaise longue*, with no back to it. On the *chaise longue* is a small, round embroidery frame with some embroidery material in it. Far right is a writing desk, on which repose a telephone, a large bell (rather like a school bell), an inkwell, a rounded blotter with a handle, some writing-paper and a couple of quill pens. Before it is a swivel stool, identical to the piano stool. Underneath, to its left, is a waste-paper basket. DR and DL, just within each proscenium wall, are two low tables, at right angles to the auditorium, on which vases will be placed. In the back wall, on either side of the C entrance, are windows with a view of snow-covered fields and a distant mill or dacha, against a night sky. (The windows are optional.) The C entrance is not a door, but a corridor in perspective, going off to some unexplained part of the house. Since there are windows on either side, it doesn't really make any sense whatsoever. (The other two entrances are also fanciful corridors in perspective.) Between the UR entrance and the UR window is a stand, or easel, on which a picture will be placed.

Characters

The performing Ushers in Act I are designated for convenience by the names of the characters that each will assume in Act II. It is recommended that each actor substitute their own name in the appropriate places in Act I, and also those of their fellow Ushers. The programme for each production should only list the names of the actors, for Act I, as members of "The Company". The role of Gino was originally played by a female.

The additional musical instruments referred to in the "It All Comes Out of the Piano" sequence were actually played by the original Cast. Other companies may prefer to substitute other appropriate instruments.

Costumes

Act I

The Ushers wear basic trousers and tops or jackets that button up to the neck (men) or skirts (and sometimes slacks, if desired) and blouses (women). Capes—short or long—may be added. Mrs Pavlenko wore a medium length one for much of Act I, and Constantine a long one occasionally. The Usher uniforms on Broadway were a basic light grey, with varying designs of military style braid in gold, red and black. All wore white gloves, unless it was absolutely necessary to take them off. All wore black boots or shoes.

Each Usher needs a pair of tap shoes, preferably gold.

Appearances on the Ankle-stage require shoes, trousers, skirts, shorts sufficient to give the impression of the character that the performer is meant to represent. This should also include jacket, coat or cape where the hem is likely to show, and contribute to the characterisation. The main demand for a variety of recognizable costumes is in the number "Famous Feet", where the characters are sufficiently described for companies to be able to use their imagination.

Act II

A good look at any Marx Brothers movie should provide sufficient reference for the design of the costumes, particularly earlier rather than later movies. Constantine's high-necked, Cossack-style shirt and high boots should add to a kind of token Hollywoodesque Russian look.

ROYALE THEATRE

Ⓢ A Shubert Organization Theatre

Gerald Schoenfeld, *Chairman* ———————— Bernard B. Jacobs, *President*

ALEXANDER H. COHEN & HILDY PARKS
present

A DAY IN HOLLYWOOD
A NIGHT IN THE UKRAINE
A MUSICAL DOUBLE FEATURE

Book and Lyrics by
DICK VOSBURGH

Music by
FRANK LAZARUS

With

PRISCILLA LOPEZ   DAVID GARRISON   FRANK LAZARUS
STEPHEN JAMES   PEGGY HEWETT   KATE DRAPER
NIKI HARRIS   ALBERT STEPHENSON

Scenery by
TONY WALTON

Lighting by
BEVERLY EMMONS

Costumes by
MICHEL STUART

Sound Design by
OTTS MUNDERLOH

Musical Direction and
Vocal and Dance Arrangements by
WALLY HARPER

Hair Designs by
JOSEPH DAL CORSO

Co-Produced by
ROY A. SOMLYO

Associate Producer
PHILIP M. GETTER

Co-Choreographed by
THOMMIE WALSH

Directed and Choreographed by
TOMMY TUNE

Original Cast Album on DRG Records and Cassettes

The Producers and Theatre Management are Members
of The League of New York Theatres and Producers, Inc.

ACT I

A DAY IN HOLLYWOOD

During the following opening number, members of the cast enter through the "lobby" doors. They exit either through the doors or into the wings

Throughout, they maintain a pride in their privileged positions as Ushers at Grauman's Chinese Theatre, in their somewhat military uniforms and with a bearing to match

Gong; House Lights dim; gong; CURTAIN *lights dim; gong;* CURTAIN *rises on:*

Song 1: The Movies Get You Through

Constantine *(alone on stage, singing)*
> Come with me to Grauman's Chinese Theatre.
> Lots to see at Grauman's Chinese Theatre
> Laugh here, cry here —
> Bid your cares goodbye here.
> You'll find
> Fantasy's what we supply here.

All Voices Off *(off)*   The movies...
> The movies...

The Ushers sing the following number, entering and exiting through the doors. All line assignments are subject to choreography, so are not indicated here

> The movies, the movies!
> That fabulous blend
> Of laughter — adventure —
> The kiss at the end.
> When your sparkle's lost its spark
> Let the movies get you through.
>
> You came in downhearted
> But after a while,
> You're caught in the story,
> You've started to smile.

Things look brighter in the dark —
Yes, the movies get you through.

The movies, the movies
Are where you go to feel grand.
Buy a one-way trip at the ticket window —
And you're in Happyland.

They fill you with wonder
They chill you with fear —
They thrill you
Until you
Could stand up and cheer.
Funny how a picture show
Seems to make your troubles go —
The movies! The movies!
They get — you — through.
The movies…
The movies…

The late great depression
Was gloomy and gray —
You needed Marlene
And Myrna and Mae!
All terrific talkie queens —
And their movies got you through.

George Raft was our fav'rite
At playing a hood.
His facial expressions
Were both very good.
And for dazzling dance routines,
There was Busby Berk'ley too!

Oh, Busby—oh, Berk'ley!
We grinned our happiest grins
When a hundred blondes wearing silk pajamas
Played neon violins!

When Gable shook Harlow
And called her a tramp,
When Garbo lay dying
Your hankies were damp.
And when lovely Alice Faye
Crooned the breadline blues away—

(The) movies, the movies!
They got—you—through.

On the last line, all march across the stage past the piano, to exit L, except Carlo, who sits at the piano. The other five Ushers re-enter immediately with shiny black cushions with designs as described below

Each cushion displays a red star on the side visible to the audience. On the side hidden from the audience three of the cushions depict the face of each of the Marx Brothers; the remaining two cushions have a gold star on each. The five Ushers proceed past the piano, UC, circling back towards L and then R across the front in a snake-like procession, displaying only the red stars on their cushions. Carlo remains at the piano, playing and singing; the other five kneel on their cushions and sing. During the next chorus, the five perform a sort of hand-jive while singing

(*Whispering*) The movies, the movies
Are where you go to feel grand.
Buy a one-way trip at the ticket window—
And you're in Happyland.

(*Building to full voice*) They fill you with wonder
They chill you with fear—
They thrill you
Until you
Could stand up and cheer.
Funny how you seemed so low
Just a picture show ago!
The movies! The movies!

Our movie's a riot—
But first if you please,
The pick of the Ushers
At Grauman's Chinese
Do their nineteen thirty-nine
Singing, dancing Valentine
To movies—
The movies
That get—you—through!

Song 1a: The Movies Get You Through (Reprise)

After applause, the melody is repeated on the piano, during which the five Ushers repeat the hand-jive, until: "And you're in Happyland". On "Happyland" the five Ushers rise, picking up cushions, still displaying red stars

           At Grauman's the movies
           Are always the best—
           The Thin Man,
           The Tin Man,
           The Witch Of The West—
           And for goofy gags and puns:
           Mrs Marx's wayward sons

On "sons" the Ushers flip the three centre cushions to reveal the faces of the three Marx Brothers, Groucho in the middle

           The movies! The movies!
           They get—you—through!

On "through!" the Ushers flip the two outside cushions, revealing the two gold stars. Simultaneously, the three centre "faces" are raised in a triangle, with Groucho at the apex, so that all five cushions form a pyramid shape. They hold in a tableau

When they break, Samovar exits R, *Gino exits* L

Carlo rises from the piano and joins the three others, and all four Ushers now remaining on stage march briefly into a line, C, *to marching music ("Mr Sid Grauman")*

During the next two lines, the traveller covering the Ankle-stage opens, revealing the legs of Mr Sid Grauman (played by a swing dancer or ASM) who has a cane. The Ankle-stage is backed by a tilted mirror, in which is reflected the floor of the Ankle-stage, paved with signed footprints like the forecourt of Grauman's Chinese Theatre

Song 2: Mr Sid Grauman
Four Ushers (*singing*) Mr Sid Grauman
                     A man with a dream!

Gong

Nina and Mrs Pavlenko exit R, *Carlo exits* L

Constantine Shortly before the opening of the Chinese Theatre, Mr Sid Grauman was watching masons— (*He turns sideways, facing* L, *and starts walking backwards, towards* R)

On the Ankle-stage, the legs of Sid Grauman do likewise

—lay the pavement in the forecourt. Without thinking, he stepped back into a block of wet cement.

On an improvised chord immediately following "cement", Constantine illustrates his narrative by stepping back as if into wet cement. He then lifts his "cement-covered" foot. "Sid Grauman" simultaneously does likewise

When Mr Grauman looked down at the footprint he had made, he suddenly got an idea.

Keeping his "wet" foot off the ground, Constantine hops forward across the stage, to music vamp, and exits L

Simultaneously, "Sid Grauman's" legs do likewise

As the vamp continues, Samovar and Gino enter from opposite sides, now wearing gold tap shoes. Simultaneously, Sascha and Masha enter on the Ankle-stage, as the legs of Dick Powell and Ruby Keeler

Song 3: Famous Feet

Samovar & Gino   Here on
Hollywood Boulevard
There's a hall of fame
Where the movie czars
And the—starriest stars
You can name
Have placed their famous feet

"Dick and Ruby" tap dance on the Ankle-stage. Samovar and Gino turn and stare at them. Then they turn back and continue singing, excitedly. "Dick and Ruby" pose

Footprints
Makin' you certain that
You ain't worth a cent—
In this town you'll find
That unless you're enshrined
In cement
You don't have famous feet

Tap break on the Ankle-stage

> Seems I stand and stare
> At those footprints out there
> About a dozen times a day.
> All the fame they've had—
> Oh, do I want it bad
> And will it ever come my way?
>
> I'll dance my shoes off
> Over and over and
> Get that break somehow!
> Tell me, what'll happen—
> These feet that I'm tappin'
> Right now —
> Will they be famous feet?

Dance break on the Ankle-stage. Samovar and Gino face UC *and watch*

  After the dance, "Dick and Ruby" exit R

Samovar and Gino face the front

> Oh—see those famous feet
> All those famous feet!

On Ankle-stage, R, *Nina enters as "Charlie Chaplin", with a cane. During the next two lines, "he" crosses* R *to* L

Simultaneously, Samovar and Gino imitate "Chaplin's" steps from R *to* L

> Oh—see those famous feet
> Love those famous feet!

  "Chaplin" exits

  The legs and skirt of Mrs Pavlenko as "Sonja Henie" on ice skates appear on Ankle-stage, L

She picks her way across the ice in unison with identical movements from Gino, to R. *Samovar watches*

Gino (*moving with "Sonja Henie"*)
> Boy, oh boy I'd like to be
> There in that
> Gallery

> Bet your life
> Your life is sweet
> When you've got those—
> (*simulating the sound of skates on ice*) Ssh! Ssh!
> Famous feet.

As "Sonja Henie" goes off R, *Constantine appears as "Tom Mix"*, L

He moves in unison with Samovar, L *to* R. *Gino watches*

Samovar (*with a Western accent*)
> Oh—see them famous feet
> All them famous feet!
> Oh—see them famous feet
> Love them famous feet!

"Tom Mix" exits R

Dance break on the Ankle-stage. Samovar and Gino watch the following procession

Nina as "Marlene Dietrich" crosses L *to* R, *dragging a chair, pauses, then exits, dragging the chair with her*

Samovar and Gino sit on the bench R *and continue watching, Gino sitting on Samovar's knee*

Masha, as a young "Judy Garland" playing Dorothy in the Wizard of Oz, skips on R, *wearing the ruby slippers*

She does a skipping dance, ostensibly along the Yellow Brick Road. She freezes R *as the music abruptly becomes ominous*

Constantine enters L *as "Dracula", wearing a voluminous cloak*

He advances on "Judy", stands behind her and stretches out his cloak menacingly. She trembles, her knees knocking together. She clicks her heels together three times. But the cloak surrounds and engulfs her, and as "Dracula" lifts her up, the Light fades on the Ankle-stage and returns to Samovar and Gino

Constantine and Masha exit L *in the darkness*

Samovar & Gino (*still sitting*)   Oh…

Lights up again on the Ankle-stage

> *"Sid Grauman" enters* L. *During the following verse he does a vaudeville dance with his cane, crossing the stage back and forth, ending* C

> > Footprints
> > Thanks to that accident
> > We can certify—
> > That from Nome to Dover,
> > They come from all over
> > And why?
> > To see those famous feet!

Samovar and Gino rise

> *During the next chorus, Mrs Pavlenko enters* R *as "Dorothy Lamour", swiveling her hips in her sarong, as she crosses "Sid Grauman" from* R *to* L. *He follows her off*

Samovar & Gino (*imitating "Dorothy Lamour" while singing*)
> > Oh—see those famous feet
> > All those famous feet!
> > Oh—see those famous feet
> > Love those famous feet!

> *Constantine appears* R *on Ankle-stage as "Al Jolson" in black, with white gloves, and goes down on one knee, clasping his hands, then spreading his hands and arms. (Of course his head is never visible)*

Samovar does likewise

Samovar (*with a Jolson voice*)
> > Two more tootsies
> > Would be fine—
> > Oh, Lawdy please
> > Make 'em mine!

> *"Jolson" exits*

> *Dance break: as Gino joins Samovar, Sascha enters* L AS *"Mickey Mouse" and Masha enters* R AS *"Minnie Mouse", both in their yellow clogs, their tails visible—"Minnie's" wears a bow*

All four now dance. At first, Samovar and Gino watch and attempt to imitate.

*As the dance builds, "Mickey's and Minnie's" steps occasionally defy
gravity—by use of the overhead bar—which Samovar and Gino are unable
to follow. The dance break ends with a "challenge" section. Then all four
dance, while Samovar and Gino sing the final chorus*

Samovar & Gino   I'll dance my shoes off
                     Over and over and
                     Get that break somehow!
                     Tell me, what'll happen—
                     These feet that I'm tappin'
                     Right now—
                     Will they be famous feet?
                     Forever in concrete?
                     Like all those famous feet?

Lights out on the Ankle-stage. Traveller closes. The mirror is removed

Samovar and Gino pose a moment, then exit L

Carlo enters and sits at the piano

          Song 4: Where Else But on the Silver Screen?
Carlo   Oh, what nights at Grauman's Chinese Theatre!
                     What delights at Grauman's Chinese Theatre!
                     Westerns, weepies,
                     Musicals and creepies—
                     You can
                     Guess that I'm a movie fan!

                     On the silver screen,
                     You hear the same clichés go by.
                     Like Bette Davis tells her guy:
                     "Yes, you're sick! And I hope
                     That you die! Die! Die!"
                     Couldn't do without them.
                     Wouldn't want to try!
                     How I love that time-honoured scene
                     That you find in ev'ry thriller—
                     Girl on the run from the psychopathic killer—
                     She hides inside the closet!
                     He's right outside the closet!
                     So what does she do?
(Speaking)   Ker-choo!

(*Singing*)   On the silver screen,
                            I love the moment when they tell
                            Poor Alexander Graham Bell:
                            "Telephone? Sorry, Al —
                            That'd never sell."
                            How I love those lines so comf'tably familiar —
                            Like "Open that safe, or I'll drill ya!"
                            Or "Doctor, please destroy your death machine!"
                            But he doesn't!
                            Where else but on the silver screen?

                            On the silver screen,
                            I like the things they say and do…

(*To the audience*) For example—(*American*) "Maybe I'm crazy, Pontius,
but there's something *about* that carpenter's son from Nazareth!"

Heads appear through portholes

And let's not forget… (*He gestures towards Samovar*)
Samovar (*dying Irish-American*) "They got me! And to think I was retiring
from the police force today!"
Nina (*English*) "I can't believe it, Clive. Only two hundred pounds for this
big, wonderful old house!"
Constantine "Go on, Sally—cry. You should have cried a long time ago."
Gino "You've got no heart! All you've got inside you is a book of army
regulations, George Armstrong Custer!"
Carlo "I'm terribly afraid we can't get through to Rangipur, Sir—all the
wires have been—*cut!*"
Samovar "You mean *you're* J G McKenzie, the new efficiency expert? But
you're a *girl!*"
Nina "You fool, Slim! Now every two-bit gun-slinger in the territory's
gonna be a-gunnin' fur you!"
Constantine "She's stopped fighting, doctor! It's as if she's simply … lost
the will to live!"
Gino "But officer, you've got to believe me—ten minutes ago the body was
right there!"
Carlo "Wait! This creature is my creation—surely I can control it!" (*He
screams shrilly*)
All   On the silver screen
                            I like the things they say and do.
Samovar   I like the stupid cowboy who
                            Says "I took me a look
                            And there ain't no Sioux!"

An arrow appears in Samovar's forehead and he falls out of sight with a gurgle

Samovar *(falling out of sight)* Aggh!
Carlo   Then there's—"Listen, cheetah! Jane in plenty trouble!"
Constantine   "It's so simple! The king must have a double!"
Nina   *(frightened Cockney)* "You're that evil friend of Doctor Jekyll's!"

Samovar comes back

Samovar   "You're *not* that little tomboy with the freckles!"
Constantine   "Watch out, Watson! Do not sniff that orchid!"
Carlo   "Me say paleface speak with tongue that's forkid!"
Gino   "Look, Professor—Chuck is turning green!"
All   "He's a martian!"
Carlo   Where else—but on the
All   Sil-ver…
Carlo *(American)* "Why, the whole thing was just a dream! (*He points to the others, one by one*) You were there—and you, and you, and you! And I love you all!"
All *(singing)*   On the silver screen!

Carlo exits as the portholes snap shut

Mrs Pavlenko enters R, carrying a mop. She wears a kimono, owlish glasses and a wig with curlers in it, suggesting a frumpy housewife who's only recently got out of bed

Song 5: A Day in Hollywood
Mrs Pavlenko   Whatever I had to eat last night
                           Before I went to bed,
                           Tonight I'll be having a double portion of!
                           I dreamed that I went to Hollywood,
                           And it's all that folks have said:
                           A lotus-land of laughter
                           And love!

                           I dreamed that I was next to Henry Fonda
                           In his custom-built Lagonda.
                           He and Gable drove me to the beach.
                           And there was Howard Hughes

And Errol and Gary—
Then came the magic moment when Cary
Begged me: "Please be Mrs Archie Leach!"

On a day in Hollywood,
Life's a song!
Fay Wray in Hollywood,
Congas with King Kong!

Then later Bing began to bub-bub-boo me—
Cagney kissed me
Disney drew me
Lugosi gave my neck—such a bite!
What a perfect day in Hollywood—
Hollywood—
Last night!

Tallulah gave a party—
Seemed kinda quiet
Till the Three Stooges
(They're such a riot!)
Took a gun and shot her in the leg.
Then ev'rybody started
Acting ka-razy—
First Donald Duck got
Dressed up as Daisy,
Then he gave a— (*She quacks*)
And laid an egg!

Ev'rything was looney there.
Picture me
With Mickey Rooney there
Dancing cheek to knee.

I heard the great director, Mr Lubitsch
Tell Joan Crawford
"Nuts to you, bitch!"
Crawford smiled and—set him alight!
What a perfect day in Hollywood
Hollywood—
Last night!

George Sanders took the floor—
I do love Georgie!

He said, "Let's all have an orgy!"
Then Mae West said "Honey, I'm your goil!"
My eyes began to pop when Lana and Hedy
Jumped into beddy
With Nelson Eddy!
Popeye shouted out for Olive Oyl!

Oh, that day in Hollywood!
Fun galore!
Charles Boyer in Hollywood
Murmured "*Je t'adore!*"

And just as I began to act like a harlot,*
David O. Selznick
Shouted "There's Scarlett!"
Signed me for the part right away!
So I made the film and was I good!
Got an Oscar too—I knew I could!
What a perfect day in Hollywood
Hollywood—
Hollywood—
USA!

Mrs Pavlenko exits L

The traveller opens on the Ankle-stage

Masha enters R *on the Ankle-stage with a suitcase, which she puts down. During the following speech, she "parades" as at an audition. She lifts her skirt modestly to show her legs in an attractive pose*

On the main stage, Constantine enters R

Constantine The beautiful hopefuls of Hollywood! From every city and small town in America, lovely young girls pour into the movie capital, drawn by the irresistible call of stardom. But though many are called, few are chosen.

Contantine exits R

Masha picks up her suitcase and exits R *dejectedly*

The travellers close

---

* pron. "harlit"

Gino enters L *on the main stage, carrying a suitcase*

Gino
                                Song 6: Tinseltown
                    Eldorado—Samarkand
                    Can't compare with Movieland.
                    Make-believe is made there,
                    Sold there.
                    This amazing neighborhood
                    Bears the name of Hollywood—
                    Plus another name
                    Just as good.
                    Call it—

                    Tinseltown.
                    Come on, let's go to sunny Cal,
                    And see that city built on bal-lyhoo…
                    Tinseltown
                    Can make an idol overnight
                    And the next one might
                    Be you…

                    You're sure you're gonna crash the big time.
                    Your special style will show—
                    And you'll see your face
                    Ev'ry place you go—

                    In Tinseltown,
                    Where nothing's ever what it seems:
                    You try to reach the moon,
                    And all
                    Too soon,
                    You see
                    Your Technicolor dreams
                    Fade away in
                    Tinseltown.

                    Tinseltown.
                    I came out West 'cause Fox had seen
                    My photo in a magazine
                    Display.
                    Well!—Blow me down—
                    They gave me this terrific deal—
                    Seven years at real
                    Good pay…

But though I made a dozen Westerns
And did a "Charlie Chan"—
I was just a flash
In the well-known pan...

I'm leaving town
And going back where I began.
I cried a lotta tears
In those short years...

But still—
At least I got a tan
From my stay in
Tinseltown.

You can keep this garden spot!
Though they love you when you're hot,
Don't expect "Hello" when you're down. (*She picks up her suitcase*)
And so, as the sun slowly sinks in the West—
We say thank you and farewell
To Tinseltown.

Black-out

During the Black-out, Gino exits L

Samovar enters through door 4

The doors are revolved by the cast so that when the Lights come up, all doors have been changed from black to red. Lights up on Samovar, wearing a floppy cap and holding a clapper-board. On it are the words "THE STORY BEHIND THE SONG"

Samovar You know, out here in Hollywood, sometimes real life can have a funny way of looking exactly like a corny movie. Here are three stories about Hollywood songwriters and every story is *true*... True story number one: the scene—a small bar near Paramount Studios, shortly after the repeal of prohibition. Enter two songwriters...

Constantine—lyricist, and Carlo—composer, enter through doors 1 and 2, respectively, and pose, C

—Sam Coslow and Arthur Johnston, tired and discouraged after spending seven hours seeking the muse in vain. Action!

Samovar claps the board, and exits, R. Simultaneously, Nina enters DL as a Hat-Check Girl

During Constantine's speech, Constantine and Carlo cross to her and mime handing her their invisible hats

Constantine It was a great idea of yours, Arthur, comin' here for a drink. We really *need* one, after trying all day to come up with a number for that new picture *Murder at the Vanities*.

Nina exits with the "hats"

Carlo Yeah, but we're all dried up.
Constantine (*Carlo's choice of words gives him a sudden idea*) "Dried up"?! Say—now the *country's* no longer dry, maybe we ought to write a *drinking* song for the picture!
Carlo Hey! That's a peach of an idea! But what'll we call it?

Gino enters as a waitress, behind the counter

Gino Good evening, Mr Coslow… Mr Johnston. How are you?
Constantine Not so hot, honey—we're stuck for a song title. Gimme a large Manhattan.
Carlo I'll take an old-fashioned.
Gino OK. Cocktails for two.
Carlo & Constantine *That's it!*

They rush to the piano. Carlo plays as both sing

Song 7: Story Behind the Song
Cocktails for Two
And maybe heaven will complete our plan
That all began—with cocktails for two!

They shake hands and freeze

Gino Gee, I'm so proud!

Gino exits

Samovar pops up behind the counter

Samovar Cut!

During Samovar's following speech, Constantine and Carlo move to join their "wives" as Mrs Pavlenko enters as Mrs Loesser through door 3 and Nina enters as Mrs Carmichael through door 4

All four pose until "Action!"

True story number two. The scene: the Hollywood home of Mr and Mrs Hoagy Carmichael, nineteen thirty-eight. Lyricist Frank Loesser and his wife are the Carmichaels' dinner guests. Action!

Samovar claps the board and exits

Mrs Pavlenko Gee, thanks, Hoagy. Frank and I had a divine time.

Constantine Yeah we really *needed* a break, Hoagy. After trying all day to write a number for Bob Hope and Shirley Ross to sing in that new picture … but we're all dried up.

Carlo Yeah, we've been seeking the muse in vain.

Nina How's about a little nightcap?

Mrs Pavlenko No thanks, honey. (*She yawns*) Frank and I are just—two sleepy people.

Constantine & Carlo *That's it!*

They rush to the piano and sing and play in quick tempo

Two Sleepy People
Two sleepy people
By dawn's early light
And too much in love to say goodnight.

Carlo stands. Both shake hands and freeze

Mrs Pavlenko & Nina Gee, we're so proud!

Samovar enters DL

Samovar Cut!

During the following speech, Nina and Mrs Pavlenko exit R

Constantine and Carlo take up new positions—Carlo slumped at the piano, Constantine standing

True story number three. The scene: the Hollywood home of songwriter Harold Arlen, Nineteen thirty-nine. Harold and lyricist Yip Harburg are seeking the muse in vain. Action!

Samovar claps the board, and exits R

Constantine paces, concentrating hard. Carlo plays a few notes, rather hopelessly

Carlo Fine songwriters we are, trying all day to finish a number for Judy Garland to sing in that new picture *The Wizard of Oz.*
Constantine That's a great refrain you got there, Harold. If only you could come up with the middle section!
Carlo It's no use, Yip, I can't come up with anything. I'm all dried up.

Gino enters as Mrs Arlen through door 5, near the piano

Gino Harold, have you fed the dog yet?
Carlo Sorry, honey, I forgot—I'll call him. (*He goes downstage and whistles the "Someday I'll wish upon a star" section of "Over the Rainbow"*)
Constantine Say, Harold! That tune you're whistling!
Gino He always calls the dog that way.

Carlo whistles again, begins adding the melody of "And wake up where..."

Carlo & Constantine That's it!!

They rush to the piano, sing and play

Over the Rainbow
Someday I'll wish upon a star
And wake up where the clouds are far
Behind me
Where troubles melt like lemon drops
Away above the chimney tops
That's where you'll find me...

Carlo (*to the audience*) Everybody!

The full cast enters and sings, encouraging the audience to join in, as the traveller opens on the Ankle-stage, revealing "Judy" in red shoes and a rainbow-lined cape, which she holds wide open

"Judy" is standing on a "step unit"; a clip-on of a perspective section of the Yellow Brick Road is attached to the front of the unit, so that as "Judy" does gentle foot movements, she appears to be hopping lightly along the Yellow Brick Road throughout "Over the Rainbow"

All   Somewhere over the rainbow
                           Bluebirds fly
                           Birds fly over the rainbow
                           Why then, oh why can't I?

Carlo They're singing it all over the world!

All   If happy little bluebirds fly
                           Beyond the rainbow
                           Why, oh why, can't...

The cast lets the audience sing "I" and applauds them

All exit, except Samovar, Constantine and Carlo

The travellers close. Carlo remains sitting at the piano. He takes out spectacles and a pipe from a hidden pocket on the upstage side of the piano, and puts on the spectacles and places the pipe in his mouth. Constantine, meanwhile, crosses to stand in the bend of the piano

Samovar (*to the audience*) Thank you, Munchkins! And now on to *another* Hollywood songwriter.

Samovar exits L

Song 7a: Hollywood Playoff

As Carlo begins to play "Hooray for Hollywood"—which he continues under the following speech—door 6 revolves, to reveal a photograph, filling the porthole, of the face of Richard Whiting, with pipe and spectacles

Constantine "Hooray for Hollywood"! Every time the lights go down before the start of a feature picture here at Grauman's Chinese, that's the music we play; and so here is our tribute to the man who *wrote* "Hooray for Hollywood", and lots of other songs we all know—from "Too Marvelous for Words" to "The Good Ship Lollipop". This composer's name? Richard Whiting.

Song 8: Richard Whiting Medley
It All Comes Out of the Piano
Mr Richard Whiting
At your piano you compose
So many hits for movie shows—
Oh, won't you tell us how?

Carlo (*as Richard Whiting*) When it comes to writing
                    I'm no professor, nosirree—
                    Still, I've a methodology.
                    Let's make it work right now.

    Constantine exits L

                    Got my fingers on the keys
                    Wandering the way they please
                    It all comes out of the piano —
                    Any old piano.
                    Sitting at the eighty-eight,
                    Sumpin' starts to percolate.
                    It all comes out of the piano —
                    Any old piano.

During the next section, from "Hey—" to "Any time", one by one each
porthole, from 6 to 1, is lowered, and as each is lowered, a hand appears; the
hands wear white gloves with black marks suggesting the black and white
keys of a piano on the fingers. The hands open and close in rhythm

                    Hey —
                    Here's a little melody
                    In A-flat major
                    Say —
                    This could be the middle of the song:
                    I'm glad I played-ja!
                    Put me at the wooden box
                    Soon a pretty tune unlocks.
                    It all comes out of the piano —
                    Any old piano
                    Any time.

The hands now do variations of "playing the piano" through the next chorus

                    Ev'ry single note I need
                    Positively guaranteed.
                    It all comes out of the piano —
                    Any old piano.
                    Never ever ask me out
                    If a baby grand's about:
                    'Cause I'll be there at the piano —
                    Bangin' your piano.

The hands disappear. The unseen cast members turn, crouching, behind the doors, and the backs of their heads and their hands appear in the portholes. The hands now "play" along the curve above the portholes

> Gee —
> Other kids were melancholy
> At the keyboard
> Me:
> I could go for hours at a stretch
> And never be bored!
> When a pair of wings I wear
> Won't be playin' harp up there.
> It all comes out of the piano —
> Any old piano
> Any time.

The heads and hands disappear

The portholes remain open, except porthole 6, which is raised again, still showing "Richard Whiting"

In the following sequence of Richard Whiting songs, the performing of them is enlivened by members of the cast bringing on assorted musical instruments which they proceed to play. (See note under "Characters" in the Production Notes on page x)

At times the piano is silent

Samovar suddenly appears on top of the piano, with a clarinet

During his clarinet introduction to "Ain't We Got Fun", the doors 1 to 5 are flipped from behind by the cast to a halfway position, so that they rest at right angles to the audience

Nina flips door 1 as she enters through it; she goes to stand at the piano, up stage of Carlo

Carlo plays the piano throughout the following number

Ain't We Got Fun

Samovar (*on clarinet only*) *"Every morning, every evening"*
Carlo (*singing*)   Ain't we got fun
Samovar (*on clarinet only*) *"Not much money, oh! But honey"*
Nina & Carlo (*singing*)   Ain't we got fun.

Samovar (*on clarinet only*) *"There's nothing surer,*
The rich get rich and the poor get poorer;
In the meantime, in between time"
Carlo & Nina (*singing*) Ain't we got fun.

For the following number, Nina drapes herself on top of the piano. Carlo
plays the piano throughout with clarinet accompaniment by Samovar

Too Marvelous for Words

Nina   You're just too marvelous,
Too marvelous for words,
Like glorious, glamorous,
And that old standby, amorous.

It's all too wonderful,
I'll never find the words
That say enough, tell enough
I mean they're just not swell enough.

You're much too much,
And just too very very!
To ever be
In Webster's Dictionary.

And so I'm borrowing
A love song from the birds,
To tell you that you're marvelous,
Too marvelous for words.

Constantine enters DL *with a ukelele, Gino follows with chopsticks, which*
she clicks à la castanets

Samovar jumps down from the piano and lines up with them

In the following number the piano is silent. Carlo and Nina simply watch
while all three sing to their own chopsticks and ukelele accompaniment.
Samovar merely holds the clarinet. During the song the three, while facing
the audience in a line, travel slowly—turning their feet in and out—from DL
all the way to DR. *They sing softly and in close harmony. The whole number*
has a very delicate effect

Japanese Sandman

Constantine & Gino & Samovar
Here's the Japanese sandman
Sneakin' on with the dew

> Just an old second hand man
> He'll buy your old day from you
>
> He will take ev'ry sorrow
> Of the day that is through
> And he'll give you tomorrow
> Just to start life anew.
>
> Then you'll be a bit older
> In the dawn when you wake
> And you'll be a bit bolder
> With the new day you make
>
> Here's the Japanese sandman
> Trading silver for gold
> Just an old second hand man
> Trading new days for old—
>
> Trading new days for old—
> Trading new days for old.

Constantine, Gino and Samovar bow and exit

Version 1

Mrs Pavlenko enters DL *with a baritone sax*

On the Good Ship Lollipop*

Carlo plays the piano throughout

Mrs Pavlenko (*singing*)
> I've thrown away my toys
> Even my drum and trains,
> I'd like to make some noise
> With real live aeroplanes.
>
> Someday I'm going to fly,
> I'll be a pilot too
> And when I do, how would you
> Like to be my crew?
>
> (*Sax only*)
> "*On the Good Ship Lollipop*"

---

*Companies may choose to perform either version 1 or version 2 of Song 13 "On the Good Ship Lollipop"

> It's a sweet trip to a candy shop
> Where bonbons play
> On the sunny beach at Peppermint Bay.
>
> On the Good Ship Lollipop
> It's a night trip, into bed you'll hop
> And dream away

(singing)

> On the Good Ship Lollipop!

Mrs Pavlenko exits through door 3 with sax

Version 2

Samovar enters as W C Fields, wearing an appropriate hat

Carlo plays the piano throughout the following number

On the Good Ship Lollipop
Samovar *(reciting to music)*
> On the Good Ship Lollipop
> It's a sweet trip to a candy shop
> Where bonbons play
> On the sunny beach at Peppermint Bay
>
> Lemonade stands ev'rywhere... *(He shudders)*

Music stops

Lemonade stands?! Godfrey Daniel, what a nauseating thought! Wouldn't touch the stuff with a pair of borrowed lips!

Mrs Pavlenko enters as Mae West. She sees Carlo, and slowly looks him and his piano up and down

Mrs Pavlenko *(meaningfully to Carlo)* Oooh! I *love* an upright!

Samovar looks around at her

Samovar *(doing a take)* Ah, my little plum! Didn't recognize you standing up!

Mrs Pavlenko (*singing and swaying sexily to music*)
　　　　　　See the sugar bowl
　　　　　　Do a tootsie roll
　　　　　　With the big, bad devil's food cake.
　　　　　　If ya eat too much—
　　　　　　Oooh! Oooh!
　　　　　　You'll awake with a … tummy ache!
Samovar & Mrs Pavlenko On the Good Ship Lollipop,

Mrs Pavlenko　　　It's a night trip.
　　　　　　　　Into bed you'll hop.

Samovar tips his hat to her. They turn to leave, he close behind her

　(*Speaking*) Is that a lollipop in your pocket?
Samovar No, I'm just glad to see you.

They move in close formation to exit DL, *singing*

Mrs Pavlenko & Samovar (*singing*) On the Good Ship Lollipop!

Mrs Pavlenko and Samovar exit

Double Trouble*

*Carlo plays the piano throughout the following number**

During vamp, Samovar and Constantine close doors 1 and 2 respectively and appear in the portholes with melodicas, on which they play the first eight bars. During this, Mrs Pavlenko reappears, without the saxophone, (which she has handed to a waiting ASM) closing door 3 and posing in its porthole while watching

Mrs Pavlenko begins to sing second "eight" in the porthole; the others play melodicas

Mrs Pavlenko　　　I've got trouble, double trouble
　　　　　　　　What a bus'ness, oo-oo
　　　　　　　　I really shouldn't suffer,
　　　　　　　　My heart is big enough fer two.

During the rest of the song, all three enter through their respective doors, which they flip back to the half-way position, and continue on stage, Mrs

*This number could be cut if version 2 of "On the Good Ship Lollipop" is used.

*Pavlenko singing to the piano and melodica accompaniment, as Samovar
and Constantine follow her across the stage*

> I can talk with them,
> I can walk with them,
> Even spoon with them.
> But I can't go on a honeymoon with them.
>
> And that's my trouble, double trouble
> I don't know what to do
> I'm as crazy as a cuckoo, from tryin' to be true—
> I'm as crazy as a cuckoo, from tryin' to be true—
> I'm as crazy as a cuckoo
> From tryin' to be true to two.

Mrs Pavlenko, Samovar and Constantine exit, DL

Gino, Nina, Constantine and Samovar enter L, *one carrying a straw hat
(representing Maurice Chevalier) which "leads" them through the
number in a spotlight from* DL *to* DR

*Carlo plays the piano throughout the following number. This number is
whistled only, not sung*

Louise

All (*whistling*)   *"Every little breeze seems to whisper 'Louise'*
> *Birds in the trees seem to twitter 'Louise'*
> *Each little rose tells me it knows*
> *I love you, love you."*

The four Ushers have travelled from DL *to* DR, *"led" by the straw hat. Now
they each turn to face the direction from which they came, passing the
straw hat down the line, until it is in position to "lead" them back again.
During the next chorus they travel from* DR *to* DL

> *"Anyone can see why I wanted your kiss,*
> *It had to be but the wonder is this,*
> *Can it be true someone like you*
> *Could love me, Louise?"*

The four freeze in tableau. Gino has the hat

Carlo plays the piano throughout the following number

Sleepy Time Gal

Constantine   Wouldn't it be a change for you and me
                               To stay at home once in a while?

The tableau unfreezes

Samovar takes the hat from Gino, and he and Nina exit L

*While Constantine stands and sings the song with simple sincerity, Gino does
a frenzied dance at double the tempo. First she appears to mime putting on
her make-up, rouging her knees and spraying herself all over with perfume,
all done with great excitement. Then she goes "partying", like a madcap
flapper of the nineteen Twenties. Her dance becomes more and more
abandoned—she twirls faster and faster and almost stumbles—until, near
the end, she is suddenly exhausted. She goes to Constantine—who is still
singing—and crawls into his arms. He picks her up; she kisses him on the
cheek then suddenly falls asleep in his arms*

                               We cabaret until the break of day,
                               I'll bet we've danced many a mile.

                               I'd like to see a movie once more,
                               They don't keep people stayin' up until four.
                               Wouldn't it be a pleasant novelty
                               To tumble in early once more?

                               Sleepy time gal,
                               You're turning night into day,
                               Sleepy time gal,
                               You've danced the evening away.

                               Before each silvery star
                               Fades out of sight,
                               Just give me one little kiss,
                               Then let us whisper "goodnight".

                               It's gettin' late 'n'
                               Dear your pillow's waitin'
                               Sleepy time gal
                               When all your dancin' is through,
                               Sleepy time gal,
                               I'll find a cottage for you,
                               You'll learn to cook and to sew,
                               What's more you'll love it I know

When you're a
Stay at home,
Play at home,
Eight o'clock
Sleepy time gal.

Constantine carries Gino off, R

As they exit, Samovar crosses behind all the doors and flips them closed

At the same time, the traveller opens on the Ankle-stage, to reveal four units of steps—each unit is a box, with two steps on either side—representing the black and white keys of a piano. A white drop behind them is divided by rows of vertical parallel lines

The legs of Sascha and Masha, wearing gold shoes, appear L, *Sascha then Masha*

Song 8a: Beyond the Blue Horizon

Carlo picks out single notes, travelling down the keyboard with one finger of one hand, then adding one finger from the other hand, so that both fingers continue travelling down the keyboard. Sascha and Masha pick their way across the "keys". This builds into:

Carlo   Got my fingers on the keys
Wandering the way they please
It all comes out of the piano—
Oh! Once I saw the dawn
While I was improvisin'
So—I came up with something
Called "Beyond the Blue Horizon".

Carlo now picks out the melody of "Beyond the Blue Horizon" with one finger only, while the feet of Sascha and Masha pick out the keys of their "piano", corresponding to the notes Carlo plays. These notes represent the melody of the following words—which are not sung:

"Be-yond—the—blue
Hor-i-zon
Waits—a—beaut-i-ful—day
Good-bye—to—things—that—bore—me
Joy—is—wait-ing—for—me"

During the song, the cast is in portholes. On the Ankle-stage, Sascha and Masha dance, their feet flying across the "keys" while behind them the drop slowly rises through the number. The vertical lines on the white drop are now seen to be the interstices between the white keys of a keyboard, as the black keys rise into view. These are followed by a dark blue sky, then a lighter blue, and finally a huge golden sun rises on the horizon

All	Beyond the blue horizon
	Waits a beautiful day
	Goodbye to things that bore me
	Joy is waiting for me
	I see a new horizon—
	(Beyond the blue horizon)—
	My life has only begun
	Beyond the blue horizon
	Lies a ri-sing—
Carlo	It all comes out of the piano—
	Any old piano—
All Except Carlo	Richard Whiting's piano—
Carlo	Any old
All	Piano
	Any
	Time!…

Black-out

During the Black-out, the cast close the portholes. The traveller closes on the Ankle-stage. The Richard Whiting portrait is removed. Carlo remains at the piano but removes the pipe and spectacles

Lights up

During the next speech, Constantine enters, wearing a white scarf, and stands at the piano with his back to the audience, as if leaning on a bar counter, facing us

On "Follow the Fleet" Nina enters through door 1, now wearing a smart Thirties white hat and gloves, and crosses to stand alongside Constantine

Carlo (*playing gentle vamp chords under*) A big ship plowing through heavy seas… In movie musicals throughout the Thirties, all the best people have sung or danced in that romantic setting. You've seen it in movies like *Shall We Dance… Born to Dance… Follow the Fleet…* And in *The Big Broadcast of 1938* when a young Bob Hope and Shirley Ross sang a memorable song by Robin and Rainger, when they played a couple, meeting again on an ocean liner, years after their divorce.

Constantine and Nina turn

Song 9: Thanks for the Memory

Constantine (*singing*)	Thanks for the memory
	Of rainy afternoons
	Swingy Harlem tunes
	Motor trips and burning lips
	And burning toast and prunes
Nina	How lovely it was.
	Thanks for the memory
	Of lunch from twelve to four
	Sunburn at the shore
	That pair of gay pajamas
	That you bought and never wore.

Constantine Say, by the way—what ever *did* happen to those pajamas?

She doesn't reply

   Huh?

Nina	Letters of sweet little secrets
	That couldn't be put in a day wire
Constantine	Too bad it all had to go haywire
	That's life I guess
	I love——

   (*Speaking*) Your dress.
Nina Do you?
Constantine It's pretty.
Nina Thanks…

The traveller begins to open very slowly on the Ankle-stage, which suggests the deck of a ship, the moon beyond the rail

	(*Singing*) For the memory
	Of faults that you forgave
	Rainbows on a wave.
Constantine	And stockings in the basin
	When a fellow needs a shave
	I thank you so much.

By now the traveller is completely open, and Masha is discovered on the

Ankle-stage, R, *in a feathery gown, representing Ginger Rogers. She is facing up stage, apparently looking out to the sea*

Nina   Thanks for the memory
                            Of gardens at Versailles

Sascha enters L, *on the Ankle-stage, in tails, as Fred Astaire. He is walking on the deck. After about three steps he sees her and stops*

Constantine   Beef and kidney pie

Ginger turns, and sees Fred. During the next section, up to "How lovely it was", they, in turn, take hesitant steps toward each other, and stop, until they reach each other

Nina   The night you worked
                            And then came home
                            With lipstick on your tie.
Constantine How lovely *that* was!
Nina Huh?
Constantine   Thanks for the memory
                            Of lingerie with lace.
Nina   Pilsner by the case
Constantine   And how I jumped
                            The day you trumped
                            My one and only ace
                            (*with clenched teeth*) How lovely it was!

Fred and Ginger now begin to foxtrot together

Nina   We said goodbye with a highball
Constantine   And I got as high as a steeple—
Nina Did you?
Constantine   But we were intelligent people
Nina   No tears, no fuss
Constantine & Nina (*as a toast*) Hooray for us

The piano plays Thanks For the Memory *while they look nostalgic*

Nina   Strictly *entre nous,* (*She turns and breaks away,* R)

On Ankle-stage, Ginger does likewise

                            Darling, how are you?

During the following speech Fred walks towards Ginger

Constantine (*walking towards Nina*) And how are all those little dreams
                          That never did come true?
Nina   Awf'lly glad I met you
Constantine   Cheerio and toodle-oo
Nina & Constantine And thank you so much.

On the Ankle-stage, Fred and Ginger draw together in a kiss, as, down below, Nina and Constantine draw apart and exit at different exits, Nina R, *Constantine* L

Carlo, who has been at the keyboard throughout, now exits, UL

No. 9a: Easy to Love

There now follows a five-minute dance between Fred and Ginger on the Ankle-stage. The dance, to the music of "Easy to Love", has the intensity of a couple who had drifted apart, but whose emotional involvement impels them together. It has the brooding quality of "Let's Face the Music and Dance". Occasionally Astaire and Rogers appear literally to dance on air, as they're able to hold on to an unseen overhead bar, and even twirl on ropes. The ship's rail is used by placing one or both feet on it (in conjunction with the overhead bar for balance) in two ways: for Fred to appear to lift Ginger over his leg, and for each dancer to appear to jump over his or her own leg

The dance begins after the kiss as Ginger breaks away from Fred. Throughout, he is attempting to coax her back to him; she feels drawn towards him, but from time to time breaks away. They dance their special brand of ballroom dancing, with dips, glides, Ginger spinning away then being held abruptly. There is a rhythmic, beguine section, which he leads; she holds back, but eventually joins in, and there are moments of intricate footwork, frequently in unison. Finally, they dance together passionately, "like old times". At the climax, each simultaneously leaps into the air, and spins— each holding, with both hands, his/her own thick, coiled rope, suspended from above, whose uncoiling causes the spinning. Then they freeze

At last—in opposition to what had passed between the couple on the main stage—"Ginger" and "Fred" exit, R, *arm in arm. As they do, the traveller closes*

Black-out

During the Black-out, the cast enters, L, Carlo through door 6

Lights up on all six Ushers grouped at the piano, Carlo at the keyboard. All are now wearing golden tap shoes. All also wear white gloves, except Carlo who has his beside the keyboard

Samovar The original lyric of *Thanks For the Memory* contained a line which offended the Hollywood censor's production code. Here's the chorus with the dirty lyric.

Song 9b: Thanks for the Memory (Reprise)
Nina & Constantine   Thanks for the memory.
Of trans-Atlantic calls —
China's funny walls
That weekend at Niagara
When we never saw the falls…

A reaction from all the others

Carlo (*rising from the piano, standing with the others and pulling on his gloves*) The censor had that changed to: "That weekend at Niagara when we *hardly* saw the falls"… Sounds dirtier, doesn't it? And now, here it is: the nineteen-thirty, Hollywood Production Code.

The six Ushers perform the following number without music but in rhythm, accompanying themselves by tap-dancing throughout. They first tap in unison for four counts of eight, before speaking

Song 10: Doin' the Production Code
All   Nudity can never be permitted
As being necessary for the plot
The effect of nudity—
On the average audience—
Is immoral.
Men   Transparent materials
Translucent materials
All   And sil-hou-e-tte
Are even more suggestive
Than expo-sure.

Excessive body movements
While the feet are stationary
Violate decency
And are wrong.

No approval shall be given to
The following words or phrases:
Alley cat … applied to a woman
Tom cat … applied to a man.

Broad … applied to a woman
Tart … applied to a woman
Hot … applied to a woman
Chippie …applied to a woman
Madam … applied to prostitution
Goose … in a vulgar sense

You can't say "in your hat"
You can't say "*hold* your hat"
You can't say "nerts"
You can't say "nuts"
Except when meaning crazy.

You can't say "pregnant"
You can't say "virgin"

You can't say "damn"
You can't say "hell"
You can't say "God"
You can't say "Gawd"
Can't say "Lord"
Can't say "louse"
Can't make a noise like *bzz*! (*They blow a raspberry*)

Impure love must not be
The subject of farce or comedy

Excessive and lustful kissing
Is not to be shown on the screen
Six seconds is the maximum length
Of a kiss in a movie scene.
And it has to be done
Simply has to be done
And it has to be done
Simply has to be done
With a closed … dry … mouth!

The treatment of bedrooms
Must be governed
By delicacy and good taste.
Which means, of course, that even though
A man and a woman are fully dressed,
If they embrace on a sofa or bed,
Then one at least of the couple must have
One foot upon the floor!

Way back in nineteen thirty
On a shining April morn
The legendary Hollywood
Production Code was born.

Oh, do the Production
Do the Production
Do, do, do, the Production
Do, do, do, the Production
Do, do, do, do,
Do, do, do, do,
Do, do, do, do, do, do, do,
Do the Production Code!

All hold the final position for a moment, then break to adopt a new grouping. Carlo returns to the piano

Samovar & Constantine Finally folks, a preview of our next attraction!
Samovar It starts here at Grauman's on Monday—
Constantine —but you can see it tonight!
Samovar Coming shortly—
Constantine —in fact, just after the intermission—
Samovar & Constantine —the Marx Brothers, in their latest movie sensation!

Carlo plays and they all sing

Song 11: A Night in the Ukraine

All   The motion picture made for your delight
                          Is *A Night*
                          In the Ukraine
                          The hit of hits
                          And you'll remember it's
                          The film they said could not be made.
                          The studio that brought you

Constantine	*Grand Hotel*!
Mrs Pavlenko	*China Seas*!
Samovar	*Tarzan* as well
All	Is soon to hitcha
	With a moving pitcha
	That'll rock the new decade.

The traveller opens on the Ankle-stage, from L *to* R

As it opens it is followed by Masha and Sascha. They are wearing trousers and coats which suggest Groucho and Chico. Each is carrying one baggy leg, suggesting Harpo is in the middle, and all "three" are moving tightly together in unison. They bounce about the Ankle-stage

> It's a smash, nothing less—
> A movie you will never forget.
> Is it big? Yes yes yes!
> Or as they say in Russia—
> Nyet nyet nyet!
> Oh, Groucho, Harpo, Chico, you're a scream—
> What a team—simply insane!
>
> The merry Marxes at their bouncy best—
> Wrecking Russia just like men possessed—
> Why it's enough to make the East move West!
> Come see *A Night in the Ukraine.*

The piano music continues under

Samovar Yes, those howl-arious, fun-tastic clown princes are back in a smile-a-minute, song-sational musical mirthquake!

Mrs Pavlenko So for the laugh-time of a lifetime, see MGM's *A Night in the Ukraine*!

Constantine Storming from the pages of *The Bear*—the best-selling play by Anton Chekhov—Russia's top gag writer!

Nina And ... just hear what one of Hollywood's greatest stars, Miss Marlene Dietrich, has to say about *A Night in the Ukraine.*

Gino runs off stage and returns in a white top hat, à la Dietrich with a cigarette in a holder and dragging a chair

Music vamp under, which ends when she poses abruptly with her foot on the chair. She puffs on the cigarette, blows out smoke

Gino Ev-wyone who comes to see *A Night in the Uk-waine*, here, at Gwauman's, should bwing thwee handkerchiefs. The seats are filthy!

Gino exits and returns immediately without the hat, chair and cigarette

Note: if the company boasts a Gino who is better at impersonating Katharine Hepburn, the following is suggested instead of the above as an alternative: Gino runs off stage and returns in a wide-brimmed, floppy hat, with a ribbon under her chin. Nina, of course, refers to "Miss Katharine Hepburn"

I'm terribly, terribly mad about the Marx Brothers, really I am, really, really. I just couldn't wait to see their new film. So I went home.

Gino exits. She returns immediately without the hat

All	What a cast!
	What a show!
	It's gonna have you glowing with glee
	Ha ha ha!
	Ho ho ho!
	And while we're on the subject—
Samovar	Hee hee hee!
All	The motion picture you've been waiting for——

On "motion picture" Sascha and Masha separate, pulling apart the legs of "Harpo". They hop back and forth across the Ankle-stage, crossing each other, each holding a Harpo-leg

	You will roar
	Till you're in pain!
	You'll howl and cackle at the knockabout—
	Shriek and bellow and guffaw and shout—
	You'll be so noisy that they'll throw you out!
	Come see *A Night in the Ukraine*!
(Speaking)	All next week!

During the CURTAIN *calls, Sascha and Masha join up again, reconstituting "Harpo", and continue hopping and bouncing. The traveller closes, to display the words "A NIGHT IN THE UKRAINE". Carlo rises from the piano and joins the line-up of all the cast*

All bow, then exit through doors and wave through the portholes

Note: in the original Broadway production, full length black-and-white photographs of each of the cast in their Act II characters were affixed to the backs of the doors during "Doin' the Production Code". In the CURTAIN calls, when all exited through the appropriate doors, each revolved their door to reveal their Act II photograph, then flipped the door half-way, for a moment, to wave at the audience, and let the door flip closed again, with the photographs as the final image before the CURTAIN fell

CURTAIN

Song 12: Entr'acte

All   Oh Groucho, Harpo, Chico, you're a scream —
What a team — simply insane!
The merry Marxes at their bouncy best —
Wrecking Russia just like men possessed —
Why it's enough to make the East move West!
Come see *A Night in the Ukraine*.

(*Speaking*) Lights! Camera! Action!

ACT II

A NIGHT IN THE UKRAINE

During the entr'acte, the Lights fade on the Curtain, *which rises in the dark and Lights bump up on the set*

Music—Fanfare (No. 13 in score)—plays as Masha, the maid, enters R, *and Sascha, the manservant, enters* L, *each carrying a vase. Simultaneously, Carlo enters from* UC, *hidden behind a large picture of the MGM lion, which he's carrying*

As Carlo comes forward, Sascha and Masha cross each other, each heading towards the opposite downstage table. Carlo arrives midway between them and stops. The sound of the lion's roar is heard. Sascha and Masha freeze, then turn to look at Carlo. Carlo waggles the picture with the roar. Then he lowers the picture, to beam at the audience. He is in recognizably Chicoesque garb

Carlo Hey!

Sascha and Masha continue to the benches, on which they place their vases. Music—Merry Villagers (No. 14 in score)—resumes under. Carlo turns the picture around, revealing a portrait of Mrs Pavlenko on the other side

Hey, Sascha! Joosta think—tonight Mrs-a Pavlenko, she's-a finally gonna go out and have-a some fun. This-a party she's-a gonna go to, it's the first time she's-a leave-a the house since she getta to be a widow.
Sascha That's right—it is.

Sascha exits R

Carlo (*to the audience*) Well, atsa da plot—now let's get on widda jokes. (*To Masha*) Hey, Masha. You know, Masha, when Mrs Pavlenko's husband, he droppa dead, it sure was some big surprise.
Masha Yes — he'd never done *that* before!
Carlo (*to the audience*) Well, if at's one of the jokes, let's get back to the plot! (*He takes the picture upstage and places it on the easel*)

Off stage we hear the well-bred voice of Mrs Pavlenko

Mrs Pavlenko (*off*) Oh Masha! Masha!

Mrs Pavlenko enters

Oh, there you are, Masha. Tell Cook I shall be dining at home this evening after all.

Masha Yes, madam.

Masha exits

Carlo Hey! Hey, wassa-a matter for you, Mrs-a Pavlenko? Tonight, the doctor and his-a wife, they give-a the biggest party since who knows-a when, and now you say you no wanna go. You craze! You might meet a *man*. Some nice, near-sighted* man.

Mrs Pavlenko Please, Carlo. The only man in my life was your late master. When Major Pavlenko died, part of me died, too.

Carlo Yeah, but you can still do lots-a living with what you got left! Sure, when you husband, he die, you plenty sad. You worse than sad, you house-broken. But atsa maybe eighteen months ago. Go on, go to the party.

Mrs Pavlenko (*sighing, sitting on the chaise longue*) No, no. I shall just sit here and do my embroidery. (*She picks up the embroidery in the frame*)

Carlo (*looking out front* c) But joosta look outa de window—de night, she's-a beautiful! Gee, I wish-a de sun was out so I could take a picture of it!

Voices are heard from the nearby party, humming "A Night in the Ukraine" slowly and soulfully in waltz time

Hey, I'm-a tell ya they have-a plenty fun at that party. Joosta listen to that!

Mrs Pavlenko stands listening to the music. She is romantically stirred by it

Mrs Pavlenko (*to herself*) That melody… What memories of Nicholas it brings back! (*She sings in plummy operatic tones in waltz time*)
>The snow was heavy, but my heart was light
>On a night——
>In the Ukraine
>He clung to me
>And then we turned to see
>The cherry orchard all in white…

Gino, a Harpoesque figure, chases a screaming Masha onstage, honking his horn and carrying a watering can. Masha runs off R

---

* "short-sighted" outside America.

Carlo Hey! Gino!

Gino runs to Carlo, puts down the watering can and offers his hand. Carlo takes it—but finds he is holding a fake hand. Gino roars with silent laughter, snatches the fake hand and dances a couple of steps of the Charleston with it. He stops, notices Mrs Pavlenko standing haughtily at front, R. He drops the hand and goes over to her. He gives Mrs Pavlenko his leg

Mrs Pavlenko Oh my! (*She pushes the leg away*) Do that again and I shall discharge you immediately!

Gino repeats the leg business. Mrs Pavlenko pushes it away

Oh, I must have my nerve tonic! (*She turns to exit*)

Gino honks his horn immediately behind her

   Mrs Pavlenko gasps and exits UR

Carlo laughs. Gino and Carlo meet, C. *Carlo puts his arm around him*

Carlo Hey! Atsa some unhappy lady. She should go to the party, she'd be the belly of-a ball.

Gino takes out a telescope, looks at the desk

Hey, what-a you see with your horoscope?

Gino replaces the telescope in his pocket, goes over to the desk and sits, picks up the ink well and drinks—then blots his mouth with the blotter

Listen, Gino, you know what I'm-a like-a to do?

Gino honks enthusiastically

At's right, I'm-a like-a to play the piano!

No. 15 Gino's Mime

Gino reacts with acute distaste, as Carlo sits at the piano, starts tinkling. To this "mime music", Gino picks up a watering can, waters the fake hand. Keeping the watering can, he picks up the hand. It comes to life

   The hand tickles Gino, driving him up stage and off C

No. 15a Carlo's Piano Solo

Carlo plays his own quirky version of Rubinstein's "Melody in F", "shooting" the keys, etc.

Carlo (*finishing, turning to the audience, beaming*) Hey!

With the applause he begins to play again: Samovar's Entrance Music (No. 16 in score)

> *Grouchoesque Serge B Samovar enters from* UC. *He marches straight to the front, acknowledging Carlo's applause, as if it were for him. He crosses to the piano, where he leans in an elaborate pose, with his cigar*

Samovar You know, that music goes straight to my heart.
Carlo It does?
Samovar Yes, and it's not doing my stomach any good either. What exactly *is* that tune you're playing?
Carlo It's-a called "Were you the one who took the blooms and left me an empty vayse?"
Samovar Shouldn't that be "vahse"?
Carlo OK. "*Vahse* you the one who took the blooms and left me an empty vayse?"
Samovar Uh, excuse me, do you mind if we start this conversation again?
Carlo No. I don't mind. Hello.
Samovar How are you?

They shake hands

Carlo Oh, same as yesterday.
Samovar How were you yesterday?
Carlo I'm-a no remember that far back. Hey, you *like-a* good music? (*He prepares to play again*)
Samovar Yes, but don't let that stop you, go right ahead and play. (*He sits on the* chaise longue)
Carlo You live around here?
Samovar No, I came all the way from Moscow.
Carlo Oh. Have a rough trip?
Samovar No, thanks, I just had one. Tell me, do you work here?
Carlo No, but the brother of my mama's other son—he does.
Samovar The brother of your mother's other son. That's you.
Carlo Hey, then I *musta-a* work here!
Samovar Tell me, has anyone in your family ever committed suicide?
Carlo I'm-a no think so.
Samovar Then why don't you go down to the Volga and break the monotony?

Carlo Well, I think about it.

Samovar By the way, what do you call yourself?

Carlo I'm-a *no* call-a myself. I'm always someplace near.

Samovar No, you don't understand. You see, in my own futile way, I'm just trying to find out your name.

Carlo Oh, my name!

Carlo shakes hands with Samovar who stands

She's-a Carlo Luigi Biondello Bonanova de Mozzarella.

Samovar How do you spell that?

Carlo Wrong every time.

Both sit on the chaise longue

Hey, I'm-a no come from Russia, I was born in Italy.

Samovar Why did you *leave* Italy?

Carlo Because I no can bring it-a with me. (*He laughs*) Atsa funny joke, no?

Samovar You just answered your own question.

Carlo What'sa *you* name?

They rise to shake hands again

Samovar My name is Serge B Samovar. My father called me Serge, what he really wanted was a new blue suit.

Carlo What do you do for a living?

Samovar You know I thought you'd never ask? (*He takes sheet music from his pocket and gives it to Carlo*) Here, do you think you can play this?

Carlo You betcha my life. (*He sits at the piano and puts the music on the stand*)

Samovar Then I can best introduce myself by singing the song that made me famous, (*to the audience*) and folks, I hope it makes you famous, too.

Song 16a: Samovar, the Lawyer

I'm Russia's leading legal brain
I'm wise to all the loopholes
And very modestly I maintain
I haven't any scroop-holes
Let's not forget my father
A lawyer too was he
In fact he shouted "I object"
The first time he saw me.
I'm Samovar the boor of the bar
A most obnoxious lawyer
I'll press your law suit while you wait
And scorch it to annoy ya

I'm a sewer who knows how to sue
You slander me and that's my cue
I'll litigate all over you.
I'm Samovar the lawyer.

Carlo   Hello, lawyer.
Samovar & Carlo Hello, lawyer—hello lawyer—
Hello, lawyer.
Lawyer Samovar.

(*Speaking*) Hey!

Samovar does a short solo dance (16b in score)

Samovar   My well-known lack of legal skill
Has ev'ryone in awe
I've broken many a woman's will
It's more fun than the law!
The first case I defended—
A poor old Muscovite—
Got fourteen years for forging checks—
And he couldn't even write!

But I haven't introduced myself—
I'm Samovar the lawyer
I once addressed the court for days
In Springfield, Illinoya
On a trifling point, I wouldn't budge.
I turned the jury's brains to fudge.
They freed the crook and hanged the judge
Don't hire me, I'll destroy ya!
So three hurrahs for Samovar

Samovar & Carlo Hurrah, hurrah, hurrah!
Carlo   Hurrah!

Samovar (*speaking; to the audience*) Now, there sits a man with an open
mind. You can feel the draft from here.
I'm Samovar the lawyer.

*Samovar holds his pose, moves to Carlo to shake hands, but misses his hand
and walks right past him. He returns, and they shake hands*

Now if you don't mind, I'd like to see Mrs Pavlenko.
Carlo (*obligingly*) Mrs Pavlenko! Right this way.

*Carlo leads him up stage. But instead of taking Samovar off stage, he stops
at the portrait and points to it*

That's her right there!

Samovar Yes, well, despite the picture I'd *still* like to meet her.
Carlo Why?
Samovar Why?

They run down stage from opposite ends of the chaise longue, *and meet* DC

That, my friend, is a secret, a secret you must keep even from your own wife.
Carlo I no got a wife.
Samovar Really, who's the lucky woman?
Carlo I'm-a no answer till you tell-a me why you wanna see Mrs-a Pavlenko.
Samovar Before I tell you, you'll have to swear an oath of secrecy. Now, raise your right hand.
Carlo No!
Samovar Why not?
Carlo You'll tickle me!
Samovar No I won't. I swear it. Shyster's Honour.
Carlo OK—then I'm on your side.
Samovar You are? Well excuse me while I change sides.

They swop places

Now then, where were we?
Carlo (*gesturing*) Well I was over there and you were over here.
Samovar And I'll bet you the view was just as nauseating.
Carlo Atsa true! Now, why you wanna see Mrs-a Pavlenko?
Samovar Hey, not so fast. Are you as trustworthy as you were before?
Carlo Before what?
Samovar Before breakfast.
Carlo I'm-a no have breakfast today.
Samovar Really, what didn't you *have*?
Carlo Well, let me see. I'm-a no have-a toast and-a butter. I'm-a no have-a tootsie frootsie ice-a cream.
Samovar Anything *else* you didn't have?
Carlo I'm-a no think so. (*Excitedly*) Wait a minute! I'm-a *think* of something else I'm-a no have!
Samovar What was that?
Carlo I didn't hear anything.
Samovar (*to the audience*) I'm afraid this story has a very unhappy ending. (*He indicates Carlo*) He doesn't die!
Carlo Atsa good! OK, now, why you wanna see Mrs-a Pavlenko?
Samovar Well, two years ago I handled a case for her husband and to make a long story short…

Carlo Oh no, if you're gonna clean it up, I no wanna hear it.
Samovar Well, if it's not dirty, I don't want to hear it either.
Carlo Me neither, I'm on your side.
Samovar You are?
Carlo Sure.
Samovar Here we go.

They change sides

So you see, Pavlenko never paid me my eighteen hundred rouble fee, and
I've got to have that money by tomorrow morning. My creditors are
threatening to send me to prison and I don't have to tell you what *that*
means.
Carlo That means they're threatening to send you to prison.
Samovar I *knew* I didn't have to tell you.
Carlo I knew it too. I'm on your side.
Samovar Shall we?
Carlo Why not?

They change places again, Samovar a bit slower

Samovar Sorry I'm late.
Carlo At's OK.
Samovar Now then, is Mrs Pavlenko in?
Carlo (*pointing* UR) Sure, in the next room there, but it's a bad time to see
her.
Samovar Well, what's a *good* time?
Carlo Half an hour with Olga, the cook.
Samovar Thanks for the tip, but when can I see Mrs Pavlenko?
Carlo I'm glad you brought that up. Never. It's my job to keep stupid boring-
a people away from her.
Samovar Please, you're speaking of the man I love! (*He poses*) Hey, I'll tell
you what.
Carlo What?
Samovar You go for a walk in the garden and I'll go in and see Mrs Pavlenko.

*Carlo is about to go and then turns and grabs the tails of Samovar's coat as
Samovar is starting off in the opposite direction*

Carlo Oh no you don't, oh no.
Samovar All right then, *I'll* go in and see Mrs Pavlenko and *you* go for a walk
in the garden.

Carlo thinks about it carefully in mid-step, then breaks L

Carlo Atsa better.

Carlo exits L, *Samovar exits* R

Mrs Pavlenko and Nina enter UC. *Nina is carrying a bunch of white, long-stemmed flowers*

Mrs Pavlenko But Nina my dear, you couldn't possibly wish for a more suitable husband than that charming Baron Trofimov. What on earth could be wrong with him?

Nina Only one thing, Mother. I don't happen to love him.

Mrs Pavlenko Sentimental nonsense! It isn't as if there is anyone you *do* love.

Nina Yes there is, Mother, I simply haven't met him yet.

Mrs Pavlenko Love someone you haven't even met! How absurd child, utterly absurd!

Mrs Pavlenko exits

Nina (*to herself*) No, Mother, it's not absurd. One day I *will* meet him and then there'll be no doubt about it—no doubt whatsoever.

Carlo comes running on, sits at the piano and plays

During the song, Nina arranges some flowers in both vases, DL *and* DR

Song 17: Just Like That
(*Singing*)

The day I meet my lover,
The birds will go
"Twitter tweet"!
Each lark and finch and plover. (*She snaps her fingers*)
Just like that I'll know.
Oh how I hope he'll hasten
To end my woe—
He'll be sweet!
I'll look into his face 'n (*She snaps her fingers*)
Just like that I'll know!
His smile will switch on the sun,
Life will be fun,
Alice in Wonderlandsome.
'Cos he'll be young and handsome
And kinda "ain't love grandsome".

Constantine enters, carrying legal papers. Dazzled by the grandeur of the
house, he stares at the room while backing towards Nina

> My heart's not out of school yet,
> But even so,
> When we meet,
> I'll smile the way that Jul'yet
> Smiled at Romeo!
> The minute that I see him…

Constantine and Nina accidentally bump

Constantine Oh, pardon me. (*He stops dead*)

The moment their eyes meet, they "know". She drops her flowers. At the same
time, he drops his papers. Carlo produces a Russian magazine, which he
starts reading

Nina Why, hello!
Constantine Hello!
Nina Can I help you?
Constantine Yes please, I'm looking for Mr Samovar.
Nina Mr Samovar?
Constantine A lawyer. I drove him here from Moscow and he left these
papers in my carriage.

During the following they pick up the items they have dropped

Nina Are you a coachman?
Constantine Yes. (*He drops his head in shame*) What I wanted to be was
a playwright, but my first play was turned down yesterday by the Moscow
Art Theatre. I suppose I was just fooling myself, imagining I had talent.
Nina Oh, but that's no way to talk! Why, you're sensitive and intelligent and
witty and kind and truthful, and I'll bet you've got a lot of writing talent.
Constantine Do you really think so?
Nina Of course I do. Don't you see? If you give up because of one little
setback, you're simply running away! And from yourself!
Constantine You're right—I see that now! Why, I'll start rewriting the first
act of my play today!
Nina Oh, good for you!
Constantine No, good for *you*—you're the one who did it. You know—I
feel as if I've known you all my life.
Nina I feel that way about you, too.
Constantine You do?

Nina Yes, but…

Carlo reacts in disgust to this dialogue and resumes his reading

Who *are* you?
Constantine I'm … Constantine.
Nina I'm … Nina.
Constantine Hello … Nina.
Nina Hello … Constantine.

Carlo reluctantly drops his magazine on the floor, turns to the piano and plays

Constantine	Well, well—my worries have fled now Presto, they left me flat. And you're the cause I admit, dear.
Nina	Well well—my heart's off its head now First it goes pit-a-pat And then it goes pat-a-pit, dear.
Constantine	One look at you and my libido So sweetly sings Do, re, mi, fa, sol, la, ti, do.
	I drifted like a boat on The briny blue Till I spied The darling that I dote on (*He snaps his fingers*) Just like that I knew!
Nina	My life was far from joyful Till I saw you By my side. Now life is girl and boyful. (*She snaps her fingers*) Just like that I knew!
Constantine	We'd make a dream of a team You're what I deem More than supremely Lovely!
Nina	And you're so stars abovely!
Constantine	And you're so turtle-dovely! You have the gentle soul of A wife so true. Be my bride And proudly I will crow, love, Cock-a-doodle-doo!

Nina   I thought you'd never ask me.

Both snap their fingers

Constantine & Nina   Just like that we knew!

They kiss

 Carlo beams at them and exits quickly

Constantine Nina, was I hearing things? Did you really mean what you said?
Nina Of course, darling, every word of it. (*She places the last flower in the vase* DL)
Constantine Then let's elope.
Nina Elope?
Constantine Tonight.
Nina Tonight?
Constantine Tonight.
Nina Oh, Constantine.

 Nina and Constantine exit L

 Samovar enters R

Samovar How about a nice round of applause for the young lovers? (*He speaks too quickly for the audience to applaud*) No? Perhaps you're right. Anyway, it's about time I saw Madam Pavlenko. It's already a quarter to nine, or eight forty-five if you like it the other way around, and if you do, you ought to be ashamed of yourself!

 Samovar exits UC

 The male voices hum A Night in the Ukraine *again as Mrs Pavlenko enters* DR

Mrs Pavlenko That tune again! Oh, Nicholas, Nicholas…

 She begins to sing, and while she sings Samovar hops across C *corridor from* R *to* L *calling* "Oo-oo!" *then, cigar in hand, enters* UC *and climbs on top of the piano, meowing like a cat*

                    The snow was heavy, but my heart was light
                    On a night

> In the Ukraine
> He clung to me…
> And then we turned to see
> The cherry orchard all in white… (*She finally turns
> and sees him. She gasps*)

Samovar (*taking her in*) Well, what do you know! Somebody wrapped a skirt around the Battleship Potemkin!

Mrs Pavlenko Who are you? And why are you smoking that vile cigar in my drawing room?

Samovar I might ask you the same question!

Mrs Pavlenko But I'm *not* smoking a cigar.

Samovar Well that's why I'm not asking it. One up to me, I think. And if it were up to you, I don't know where we'd be, and speaking of you, you remind me of my younger sister, which is strange because you look more like my older brother. And speaking of my brother, why don't you? You haven't mentioned him once! I suppose you think he's not good enough to talk about! You hate my brother, don't you? You'd like to see my brother six foot under, wouldn't you?

Mrs Pavlenko Why no, of course I wouldn't.

Samovar Oh, that's nice. My brother a coal miner and you don't want him to make a living!

Mrs Pavlenko I don't under——

Samovar Will you let me get a word in edgewise? Talk, talk, talk! Why don't you have your tongue painted to match the wallpaper?

Mrs Pavlenko is open-mouthed

Why you *did*! Who are you—anyway?

Mrs Pavlenko I am Madam Pavlenko.

Samovar What, *you're* Madam Pavlenko? Why, they never told me you were young, beautiful and charming.

Mrs Pavlenko (*flattered*) Well——

Samovar And now I know *why*!

Mrs Pavlenko I see! And who may you be?

Samovar My card, madam. (*He hands her his card*)

Mrs Pavlenko (*reading*) "Serge B Samovar, lawyer. Juries bribed while you wait. G. M. T. C. B. C." What does G. M. T. C. B. C. stand for?

Samovar "Give me the card back Chubby." (*He snatches back the card*)

Mrs Pavlenko Mr Samovar, why are you here?

Samovar Why am I here? Why are any of us here? I'm too young to worry about such morbid things. I want gaiety, laughter, dancing, romance — whee — with a hi-dee-ho and a ha-cha-cha. (*He dances round her, finishing up on the chaise longue*)

Mrs Pavlenko Sir, you shake my sanity!

Samovar No, you shake mine, it's looser.

Mrs Pavlenko Mr Samovar. You are in my home uninvited and unless you leave immediately I shall ring for my footman.

Samovar (*leaping up again*) Why? Is he too lazy to ring for himself? You know, that's the trouble with footmen these days, they're all lazy. Why, when I was a footman I used to work twenty-five hours a day.

Mrs Pavlenko How could you possibly work twenty-*five* hours a day?

Samovar I used to get up an hour early!

Mrs Pavlenko goes to the desk and rings a bell at length

Mrs Pavlenko Well?

Samovar Beautiful, I didn't know you played.

Mrs Pavlenko I mean, have you anything to say before you leave?

Samovar Yes, I'm staying. (*He sits on the* chaise longue) I refuse to budge until I get my money.

Mrs Pavlenko Money? What money?

Samovar The money your husband owed me, of course. Eighteen hundred roubles.

Mrs Pavlenko If Nicholas owed you money, you will certainly be paid, but not tonight.

Samovar But it's *got* to be tonight! If I don't have that money by tomorrow morning, I'll be sent to prison and I hate living with relatives. Oh, the shame of it! You should have heard my poor old mother sob this morning when they took away her bed.

Mrs Pavlenko She was upset?

Samovar She was in it!

Mrs Pavlenko Will you please allow me to speak? My steward will return from town the day after tomorrow. You will be paid then and not before. Do I make myself plain?

Samovar Well, *somebody* certainly does.

Mrs Pavlenko I refuse to listen to another word!

Samovar Then get out of here.

She turns to leave

Both of you!

Mrs Pavlenko Oh!

Mrs Pavlenko sails out

Carlo enters L

Carlo Hey, boss, what happened with Mrs Pavlenko?

Samovar She absolutely refused to give me the money. You know, I've got a good mind to sit down and write her an angry letter!

Carlo (*running to sit at the desk*) Atsa good idea, I help-a you.

Samovar Why, do you take dictation?

Carlo Well some-a-times I'm-a take it, and some-a-times I'm-a leave it alone... Ready?

Samovar Ready. "To whom it may concern. Dear Whom. I most strongly protest about your high-handed attitude of a few moments ago, comma... "

Carlo How do you spell comma? With a C or a K?

Samovar Yes.

Carlo OK.

Samovar "And unless I receive an immediate *ipso facto*, (*to the painting*) or in your case, Madam, ipso *fatso*, I shall be forced to take the following unpleasant measures, dash..."

Carlo Sure!

Carlo leaps up and dashes off UL

Samovar Well, I've got no-one to blame but myself, I did say dash. My tongue ran away with my brain—and what they see in each other I'll never know.

Carlo enters with a sandwich

Carlo Hey, boss—I'm-a go to the kitchen, make-a myself a nice-a sandwich.

Samovar All right, let's carry on. Pull up a chair and sit down.

Carlo It's-a garlic sausage and gorgonzola.

Samovar All right—pull up a *window* and sit down.

Carlo crosses to the desk, throws the sandwich into the waste paper basket, and sits at the desk

Carlo OK, now, where we was?

Samovar Oh, I don't know, let's start over. Ready?

Carlo Ready.

Samovar throws himself on the chaise longue *in a girlish pose*

Samovar "Dear Madam, I am seventeen and considered quite pretty. However, I'm terribly shy with boys. Every time I see one, I rush home and hide under the bedclothes. What should I do? Signed, Worried Brown Eyes". Now read that back, will you?

Carlo OK. (*He reads*) "Dear Worried Brown Eyes, I'm-a very gladda you wrote-a me. If you wanna cure-a you shyness, next time you hide under the bedda-clothes, take-a the boy with-a you." Hey, you wanna add something?

Samovar (*rising*) Yes, take this down. "Finally madam, it behooves me at this juncture to state most emphatically that unless"——

Gino on one roller skate chases Masha across the stage from UR *to* DL, *honking his horn. They both disappear*

Was that an optical illusion or am I seeing things?

Carlo Atsa my brother.

Samovar Well, he ruined my flow.

Carlo Maybe your Flo, she no run fast enough.

Samovar May I see the letter?

Carlo hands the letter to him, he studies it gravely

Carlo What do you think, boss?

Samovar My friend, if you ever decide to leave your employment here and seek work elsewhere, I want you to feel free to avoid me like the plague.

Carlo Fine. What's-a that mean?

Samovar It means I wouldn't touch you with a ten foot pole. And neither would Igor Krasnapolski.

Carlo Who's he?

Samovar He's a six foot Pole. (*To the audience*) You pay your money, you take your chances. (*He gives the letter back to Carlo*) Here now, take this, type it out, and then type it back in again.

Carlo sits at the piano and puts the letter on the music stand

Meanwhile, I'm going to the kitchen and over-eat.

Carlo Atsa good idea. Today the cook, she make Hungarian galoshes.

Samovar The cook, eh? Tell me, is that the cook you recommended in a previous scene?

Carlo At'sa right, Olga.

Samovar Olga! You know, I once had a girlfriend named Olga. She lived over in Kiev, and every weekend, I'd jump into my balalaika and go visit her.

Carlo But a balalaika, atsa musical instrument.

Samovar No wonder it took me so long.

Samovar sings, as Carlo plays

Song 17a: Samovar Exit
I've broken many a woman's will
I'm Samovar the shnorrer!

Samovar exits with a "Whee!"

Carlo Hey, at-sa good! (*He lays the music stand flat*)

Gino enters, whistling excitedly

Carlo Hey, whassa matter?

Gino runs around the room, scattering confetti from his pockets. Carlo runs after him

Hey, what do you do? Gino, you make-a the mess!

Gino whistles triumphantly

Mess?

Gino then starts scratching

And now you scratch-a youself. Whassa matter—you itch?

Gino nods, whistles and honks, then scratches and throws confetti, again and again

Itch… mess … itch … mess … itch … mess … itch … mess…
(*triumphantly*) *Mess-itch!*

Gino whistles and honks, and they embrace twice, rapidly, first to the left, then to the right

Who's-a the message from?

Gino, followed by Carlo, goes to the portrait. Gino points to it

Ah! Message from-a you finger!

Gino looks at his finger, shakes his head, covers his hand with his coat sleeve and points again

Message from-a the pitch!

Gino shakes his head, pantomimes the girth and dignity of Mrs Pavlenko

   Atsa Mrs Pavlenko!

Gino honks and whistles approval. They shake hands

   OK. What's-a the message about?

Gino tries to lift Carlo

   Hey, whadda you do? Come on, be careful, you strain-a youself!

Gino whistles encouragement, honks his horn, then over the next few attempts, tries cutting off Carlo's speech by putting his hand over his mouth

   Strain-a youself?

Gino honks

   Strain-a youself… Strain-a youse… Strain-a you… Strain-a… Strain!

Gino honks encouragement

   Strain. Something about a strain!

Gino points to his jaw

   Strain-face?

Gino registers "no", points to his jaw again

   Strain-chin?

Gino registers "no", mocks a punch to the jaw

   Strain-jaw?

Gino honks

   Strain-jaw!

Gino honks excitedly

   Atsa message from Mrs-a Pavlenko about a *stranger*!

They shake hands

  OK, Gino—who's-a de stranger?

Gino puts a finger under his nose to illustrate a moustache

  Stranger with a head cold!

Gino registers "no," puts two fingers under his nose

  Stranger with-a *two* head cold!

Gino goes to strangle Carlo

  All right, all right, it's Samovar. Samovar, the lawyer!

Gino whistles, honks excitedly

  What we supposed to *do* widda Samovar?

Gino starts to eject Carlo forcibly

  Hey! Whadda you do?… Oh, we throw out Samovar! But *how* we throw-
a him out?

*Gino mimes locking a door, a bird flying, and digging. Carlo suddenly looks
triumphant*

  Ah! I don't get it! Do it again.

Gino mimes locking a door

  First you lock-a the door.

Gino honks approval

  Next…

Gino mimes a bird flying

  A chicken…

Gino whistles "no"

Not a chicken...

Gino illustrates a larger bird

   Turkey!

Gino illustrates a large flying bird, standing on the chaise longue

   Eagle!

Gino desperate, takes out a doll in diapers from his pocket, suspends it from his mouth and mimes flying again, on one leg

   Stork!! Atsa stork!

Gino honks his enthusiastic approval. He comes next to Carlo, and rocks the "baby" in his arms, while Carlo hums a lullaby. Suddenly Gino finds his hand is "wet", puts the doll in his pocket with the other hand and wipes his "wet" hand on Carlo's jacket; they mime a mock fight which Gino wins by kicking Carlo in the posterior, even though they face each other; Carlo throws a wild punch simultaneously and misses

   Hey! Come on... You kick-a my brains out! OK, now, how we throw out-a Samovar?

Gino does the door-locking business

   First, you lock-a the door.

Gino repeats stork flight business, without standing on the chaise longue

   Next a stork...

Gino mimes digging a hole and continues throughout Carlo's speech

   Then you dig-a the sand... Dig-a the earth... Dig-a the mud... Dig-a the hole... Dig-a the grave...

Gino honks his horn

   Grave! Grave... I got it, I got it! We throw out-a Samovar, *lock stork and burial*!

Gino throws a shower of confetti and collapses into Carlo's arms

Carlo drags him backwards toward the exit, L, *when Nina and Constantine enter* R

Carlo and Gino instantly take up conspiratorial positions, and watch

Constantine Then it's all settled.
Nina Of course, darling. I'll just run upstairs and pack.
Constantine Wonderful.
Nina So are you.

They kiss

Nina exits

Constantine Oh boy!
Carlo Hey boss, we eaves-a-droop! (*He goes to Constantine*)

Gino follows him

You marry Miss-a Nina right away?
Constantine Yes, we're eloping. Isn't it marvelous?
Carlo Well you know what-a they say. The heart she's only a muscle, so when you get married you not-a really in love, you just-a musclebound. (*He laughs*) I don't get it.
Constantine Well, I'm really in love with Miss Nina. Why, she's even given me the confidence to rewrite my play.
Carlo Hey, you write a play!
Constantine Yes! (*He takes out his play*) It's called *The Fortune Hunter*. Let me tell you about it.
Carlo Go ahead. (*He sits on the piano stool*)

Gino crosses L, *sits, takes out popcorn, eats it, greedily. Constantine puts his foot on the* chaise longue

Constantine It's about an unscrupulous, impoverished young nobleman who'll do anything for money. In the second act he has a very powerful scene, when he says to his friend Grischa … (*he reads*) "That's right, my friend—Anna Platov, the daughter of the rich landowner, has fallen helplessly in love with me."

Nina enters, smiling, wearing a fur coat and carrying a suitcase, and listens, unseen by Carlo and Constantine

"She and I are to be married as soon as possible. Of course I don't love the

little fool. She thinks I do, but then, as a ruthless fortune hunter, it's my
business to be convincing, isn't it?" (*He laughs callously*)

Nina drops the suitcase. From the sound, we know it's empty

Nina Constantine, how could you?
Constantine (*realizing*) Oh Nina, let me explain!
Nina No explanation is necessary, I heard everything!
Constantine But darling, you don't understand—it was only a…
Nina Get out! (*She slaps him*)

*Carlo, who has been watching, turns to the keyboard and begins to play the
introduction to* Again

    Constantine exits DL

Oh, Constantine, you've broken every bone in my heart!

*Carlo plays. While Nina sings, Gino attempts to cheer her up. He offers her
popcorn, then takes out a lollipop*

Song 18: Again
Again
I'm crying
I'm aching, throbbing,
Shaking, sobbing,
Sighing—
Love is dying
Again!
No hope for me now.
Again I'm on the shelf
And up a tree now.
All at sea now
Again!
His eyes were dark and dreamy—
'Twas so sun-beamy
Then!
But now there's heart ache.
I know I'll feel the smart from Cupid's dart ache…
Again and…

*The music continues. Nina is touched, emotion overcomes her, and she
collapses on the* chaise longue, *sobbing*

Constantine enters DL

Gino exits

Carlo picks up his magazine and begins to read

Constantine Nina, if you'd only let me explain!
Nina I told you before, there's nothing to *be* explained! Now get out!

Nina slaps him again and runs off UR

Constantine Darling, come back! Oh, Nina, it could have been so *swell*! (*In despair, he flings the playscript on to the* chaise longue *and moves towards* CL *near the piano, taking up a stance to begin singing*)

Carlo hastily disposes of the magazine on the floor and plays

> Again forsaken!
> By grief I'm overwhelmed and overtaken—
> Stirred and shaken—
> Again!
>
> Such em-ptiness now!
> Without your love I'm just an empty
> Mess now—
> In distress now—
> Again!
>
> Oh why oh why oh why, love
> And when oh when oh when
> Will gloom depart, dear?
> Why, you're so sweet that I could eat
> Your heart, dear
> Again and again!
> Again again again
> Again again and again and
> Again and again!
> Again again again
> Again again again again
> And yet
> Again and
> Again and again!

Constantine exits DL

Carlo, exhausted, shakes his fingers as if to get the circulation flowing again

Masha, the maid, runs in from L *screaming, apparently being chased by Gino*

Carlo goes off L, *attempting to head off Gino and calm him*

Carlo (*as he goes*) No, Gino! No!…

Masha heads for the exit UC, *retreats and disappears* R, *when Gino enters from* UC, *riding a very dilapidated bike*

Gino falls off the bike. He rises from the floor, gingerly touching various areas of his body which were injured in the fall from the bike, wincing as he does so. He leaps to his feet in sudden concern for any injuries the bike may have. He rights it, strokes it comfortingly. He takes a carrot out of his pocket and offers it to the bike. He stands and waits for the bike to eat it. When it doesn't, he pockets the carrot and, concerned for the bike's health, turns it upside down to examine it. He takes a stethoscope from his pocket and uses it to listen to the back wheel, pedals, and finally, front wheel. He pockets the stethoscope and takes out a small hammer. He tests the bike for reflexes by tapping the back wheel. Then he taps the front wheel, accidentally plucking one of the spokes. A single note of a harp is heard. Gino reacts to the sound. He taps and plucks again, repeating the sound. He pockets the hammer and, a look of joyous wonderment on his face, sits on the overturned bike, facing the front wheel. He "plays" the front wheel to a taped harp solo of "Again"(No. 19 in score), playing the last note on the back wheel

Gino rises, picks up the bike tenderly, bows in the grave manner of a concert soloist, and exits with the bike, L

Samovar enters, C

Samovar Hello again. Again?
(*Singing*) Again I'm crying…
(*Speaking*) No, I think we've had enough of that. (*He sees the confetti*) I've seen dandruff, but this is ridiculous! (*To the audience*) Welcome to Act One, Scene Two, knit three, purl four, in which Granny walks into the forest fire on her two wooden legs and burns to the ground. And in which Uncle Sebastian, the lovable old body-snatcher, comes to the shocking— nay, horrifying realization…

Constantine enters DL

Constantine Excuse me.

Samovar Certainly, it's the second door on the left... "Comes to the shocking, nay, horrifying..."

Constantine Mr Samovar, please, I must have a word with you.

Samovar Oh very well, Treplev, go ahead.

Constantine Thank you, you see...

Samovar That's *four* words. "Comes to the shocking, nay, horrifying..."

Constantine Will you please shut up!

Samovar Treplev, you're getting above yourself and if you fall off yourself, don't come crying to me!

Constantine I'm sorry sir, I know I'm acting strangely...

Samovar I hadn't noticed you were acting at all. Oh, very well. What's the matter?

Constantine Well, it's kinda personal.

Samovar Then I promise not to listen. (*He turns up stage, whistles and hops on one foot*)

Constantine Well, I was engaged to Mrs Pavlenko's daughter, but now she says it's all over.

Samovar What? You mean she's broken her engagement to a boy with your looks, charm and singing voice?

Constantine That's right.

Samovar Seems reasonable to me. (*He faces the front*)

Constantine That's why I'm going back to Moscow immediately.

Constantine turns and exits, Samovar trying physically to hold him back, but failing

Samovar What, and leave me stranded? But you can't leave, do you hear— you *mustn't* leave! (*He calls after him*) I forbid you to leave! (*To the audience*) I thought he'd never go! (*He sees the play on the* chaise longue, *crosses to it and picks it up*) Why, what's this? Seems to be a play. Well, as this is National Read a Play Aloud Week, I'll *read* it aloud! (*He lies on his back on the* chaise longue, *one leg in the air, and reads*) "That's right, my friend—Anna Platov, the daughter of the rich landowner, has fallen helplessly in love with me."

Nina enters to C

"She and I are to be married as soon as possible. Of course, I don't love the little fool"——

Nina What's that you're reading? Let me see! (*She takes the script from Samovar*) Why, it's Constantine's play! He was only...

There is the sound of retreating hoof-beats

What's that? Who's leaving?

They both rush DC, *to look out of the "window"*

Samovar My coachman Treplev. He just left for Moscow.
Nina Constantine gone? Oh, I can't believe it!
Samovar Try hard, it helps the plot.

Nina runs off up stage in tears

Samovar lopes to the phone and picks it up

(*Into the phone*) Hello, vice squad? Send some over! (*He hangs up, drops the phone in the waste paper basket, and begins to exit* UR)

Carlo rushes in C, *sees Samovar and points to him forcibly*

Carlo Hey Samovar! Hey! It's *you*!
Samovar (*coming a little closer to Carlo*) Tell me, did you ever say that to anyone and it *wasn't* them?
Carlo (*after some consideration*) Atsa for you to know anda me to find out.
Samovar Well I think it's about time I insulted Madam Pavlenko again, so if you'll excuse me, I'll… (*He starts to exit*)

Carlo grabs him by the tails on his coat

Carlo (*bellowing*) Hey Gino, Samovar, he's-a here! I stall-a him till you get-a here!

Carlo pushes Samovar to the chaise longue, *where they both sit*

Say, I'm-a forgetta to ask you! What did you think of Olga, the cook?
Samovar Why, she's the wildest creature I've ever met, outside of a man-eating tiger. And *inside* of a man-eating tiger I've never met *anyone*. (*To the audience*) Well, they can't *all* be gems, you have to expect that every once in a while. (*To Carlo*) Now, if you'll excuse me… (*He starts to exit*)

Carlo once again grabs him by the coat-tails

Carlo Hey, Gino, Samovar, he's-a here! I stall-a him till you get-a here!

Again they sit

You know what I'm-a like to do? I'm-a like to sing-a you a song. (*He crosses and sits on the piano stool*)

Samovar What song?

Carlo I don't know, any song. You name it, an' I sing it.

Samovar All right, what about *Sweet Sue*?

Carlo I don't know it.

Samovar *Melancholy Baby*?

Carlo I don't know it.

Samovar Then how about *When I was nine and you were eight and we were seventeen*?

Carlo I don't know it.

Samovar Now wait a minute, you said if I named it you'd sing it.

Carlo Yeah, but you ain't *named* it yet.

Samovar (*rising*) Now if you'll excuse me…

Carlo grabs his coat-tails again

Carlo & Samovar Hey, Gino, Samovar, he's-a here! I stall-a him till you get-a here!

> *Gino enters from* UC, *honking his horn and eating a banana, which he holds out in front of him. He stops between Carlo and Samovar*

Carlo (*proudly to Samovar*) Hey, you know who that is?

Samovar I don't even know *what* that is. But it looks like something a stone just crawled out from over.

Gino zips up the banana and pockets it

Carlo Atsa my brother.

Samovar Your brother, eh? Well, if your parents ever decide to sue the stork, I'll handle the case. (*To Gino*) Tell me, sir, as an outsider, what are your views on the human race?

Gino does a "gookie" look, by crossing his eyes, puffing out his cheeks, with his mouth open like a goldfish

Could you expand on that?

Gino does an even more exaggerated "gookie" look while spreading his body grotesquely. When he has made his effect he straightens up and remains completely blank and immobile throughout the following

(*To Carlo*) Hey, suet-head, remind me, why did you call your brother in here?

Carlo takes Samovar aside

Carlo (*whispering confidingly*) It's so him and-a me can take-a you by surprise and throw-a you out.

Samovar strikes a sparring pose

Samovar Throw me out? So that's your little game, is it? Well, nobody throws Serge B Samovar out! I'm going to collect that money tonight if it takes me all year.

Carlo But Mrs-a Pavlenko, she say we *gotta* throw you out.

Samovar Well I'm not going, so take heed!

Carlo When?

Samovar Three times a day after meals... Keep on with the ointment as well... Next patient! (*He moves to left of Gino*)

Carlo moves to Gino's right. Samovar hums, taking hold of Gino's arm. He takes his pulse

   (*To the audience*) Why is it they always come to me when it's too late?

Gino suddenly gives Samovar his right leg, but remains blank. Samovar stares at it, stares at Gino, taps the knee of the leg he's holding. Gino's right hand flies out and hits Carlo on the arm

Carlo Hey!

Samovar repeats this, Gino repeats it. Carlo smacks Gino on the shoulder in protest. The business is repeated until a rhythm is built up, which leads into the Anvil Chorus, *sung by Samovar, accompanied by the business and accentuated by the horn from Gino and "Hey!" from Carlo*

Samovar (*moving downstage*) That last number was a request, from Mrs Albert Scrimshaw, who is celebrating the tenth anniversary of her twenty-ninth birthday.

Carlo (*whispering to Gino*) Listen, Gino, he's-a some tricky fella. You watch-a him like a hawk.

Gino puts on a false beak and stares at Samovar

   OK, OK. Atsa good. Now we getta plenty tough!

Gino puts the false beak in his pocket, and pumps himself up to be "tough", encouraged by Carlo. Gino conveys fearsome anger, panting through clenched teeth. They advance on Samovar, who retreats in alarm

Samovar See here, you boys aren't *really* going to throw me out, are you?
Carlo Sure, and don't try to bribe us neither.
Samovar Who said anything about bribes?
Carlo Me. *Someone* had to break-a the ice.
Samovar Oh I see, you boys are interested in money, are you?

Gino greedily rubs his hands together

Carlo Sure, money, that's our second favourite subject.
Samovar What's your first?
Carlo Same as yours.
Samovar Why you filthy beasts! Now, let's get this straight, what happens if I don't bribe you?
Carlo Well, first we hitta you over the head... Bing... Bang... Bong...

Gino hits himself with a blackjack

Then we pick-a you up.

Gino reaches behind his neck and grabs his own collar

We dragga you down to the river and we throw-a you in.

Gino drags himself to the chaise longue, *throws himself over behind it, from where he hurls water into the air*

Samovar I see. And if I *do* bribe you?
Carlo Then we do all that to Mrs Pavlenko.
Samovar What, old Blubberhips? Good thinking, Mozzarella!

All three dash up to the portrait and start pelting it with flowers, etc.

Mrs Pavlenko enters UC

Mrs Pavlenko What in the world!

All freeze

Samovar Ah, Madam Pavlenko, there's no-one I'd rather see! In other words, I'd rather see no-one.

Mrs Pavlenko glares at Carlo, who begins to retreat

Gino runs out

Carlo picks up two quills from the desk and backs away as Mrs Pavlenko advances, past the portrait and the desk, round the chaise longue and then towards the piano

Mrs Pavlenko Carlo, this is all your fault. Yours and nobody else's!

Carlo retreats, and just as Mrs Pavlenko reaches him, holds out the two quills in front of him, crossed as if to ward off a vampire. This stops Mrs Pavlenko, who gasps in outrage

This room is an absolute shambles and that horrible man is still here!
Samovar I'm still here because I haven't been paid yet.
Mrs Pavlenko I'm not talking to you.
Samovar And don't think I don't appreciate it.
Mrs Pavlenko This is ridiculous! Carlo, fetch my coachman, my stable-boy and all my farmhands!
Carlo OK, lady! Good-a-bye!

Carlo exits

Mrs Pavlenko There! Soon he'll return with two dozen powerful men!
Samovar I doubt that! There're only eight of us in the cast!
Mrs Pavlenko Wretch... Scoundrel... Guttersnipe!
Samovar Go on—you're getting warm.
Mrs Pavlenko Rapscallion!
Samovar That's it! Of course, you realize this means war! Madam, I hereby challenge you-all to a duel, suh!
Mrs Pavlenko And I accept!

Gino enters with a broom to clean up the mess, and sweeps Samovar up and down with the broom

Samovar That's what I like about him, he treats me like dirt. (*To Gino*) Where are the guns?
Mrs Pavlenko (*to Gino*) Quickly, two guns!

Gino gives the broom to Samovar and produces two buns out of his pockets

Not buns. Guns! (*She explains*) Pistols! I want two pistols!

Gino nods eagerly, throws the buns away and produces two crystal ornaments

   No, they're crystals! Pistols!

Gino puts the crystals away

   The noisy things that shoot bullets! You know what a *bullet* is, don't you?

Gino nods eagerly and pulls out a very real-looking pullet in a shower of feathers. Mrs Pavlenko gives a gasp of revulsion

   (*Desperately*) I don t want a pullet!
Samovar All right, then push it!!

   Carlo rushes in L

Carlo Hey, Mrs-a Pavlenko! I'm-a hear everything! Your husband, he keep
   his-a pistols in his wall safe! (*He rushes to the piano*)
Mrs Pavlenko Splendid!

Carlo plays. During the short song, each of the three men keeps time in his own way; Gino, sitting on the chaise longue, *holding out the pullet and making its legs move with his own*

Song 20: A Duel! A Duel!
A Duel! A Duel!
We're going to fight a duel!
To shoot that scoundrel is my one desire!
Samovar (*playing the broom like a bass fiddle*) To hell! To hell!
I'll send her straight to hell—
And then the fat'll really be in the fire.
   (*Speaking to the audience*) They don't write 'em like that any more. (*He sweeps confetti*)

Mrs Pavlenko crosses to Samovar. Gino leaves the pullet on the chaise longue *and stands so that Mrs Pavlenko is between Samovar and Gino*

Mrs Pavlenko And now I shall fetch two pistols and return immediately!
Samovar Well, if you're in a hurry, why don't you travel on this?

Samovar hands her the broom, she gasps and hands it straight back. Gino gives her his leg

Mrs Pavlenko Don't *do* that!

Mrs Pavlenko exits

*Gino gives a rude honk on his horn, immediately behind her. During the
following speech, he throws confetti in the air, which he attempts to sweep,
and Carlo plays Tchaikovsky loudly on the piano (No. 21 in score), using a
foot on the keyboard*

Samovar (*pacing about and speaking through the ensuing bedlam*) From
the beautiful Cirrhosis Room high atop the lovely Hotel Bubonic in
downtown Stubenville, Ohio, mildew capital of the world, we invite you
to listen to the sounds of Guy Lombago and his over sexed-tet. This
program is brought to you by the makers of Whizzo, the suppository of the
stars!

Carlo jumps up from the piano and runs over to Samovar, followed by Gino

Carlo Hey boss, why you wanna fight a duel?
Samovar Because hell hath no fury like a Samovar scorned—except
February which hath twenty-eight. Also I resent her lying to me. That story
about her having to wait for her money until her steward gets back from
town—why I bet she's broke!

Carlo laughs, and Gino does the same thing silently

Carlo That's-a good, Mrs-a Pavlenko broke! Why, she own maybe six
whole forest. Why every time she take a breath she make a thousand
roubles. And when she take a little-a short breath like-a this— (*he
demonstrates*) she make-a five hundred.
Samovar Hey, if she ever got asthma, she could rule the world! Now, if I
could just get my hands on a piece of that money, I could change my name
from Serge to Cashmere.
Mrs Pavlenko (*off*) Out of my way!
Samovar Here she comes. Look, could you play something suitably
romantic?
Carlo Sure, boss. (*He whispers to Gino, and rushes to the piano*)

Gino dives under the piano and disappears behind it into a corner

Samovar Good, I'll tell you when.

*Samovar throws the broom off stage as Mrs Pavlenko enters from the
opposite direction with two duelling pistols*

Mrs Pavlenko Here are the pistols. Have you anything to say before we begin?

Samovar Yes I have! Ah, Natasha, all my life I've been looking for a wife like you and now I've found you, and if no-one calls for you in thirty days, you're mine.

Mrs Pavlenko You silly boy, pull yourself together.

Samovar No, you pull yourself together—you're spread out further than I am! Can't you see you're the woman for me?

Mrs Pavlenko Rubbish!

Samovar All right then — the rubbish for me.

Mrs Pavlenko Mr Samovar, you're teasing me, and I can't stand a tease.

Samovar Then stand at attention. Oh Natasha, it's all so simple. I want to marry you and you want to marry me, and I figure if we marry each other, we can do it with one wedding. Don't fight it, my sweet! (*He leads her to sit on the* chaise longue. *To Carlo*) Now… (*He turns to kneel before her, and falls on the floor. He picks himself up, and sits on the* chaise longue)

Carlo plays

Song 22: Natasha
The scent of the sweet hibiscus, dear
Is making me feel promiscus, dear.
On such a night how can you speak of du-els?
I'm gazing into your azure eyes
And no other woman hazure eyes—
No honestly, they're just like limpid poo-els.
(*Speaking*) They're the most watery eyes I've *ever* seen!
(*Singing*)   Natasha—
You're the fairest of all your sex!
Natasha—
Love your red lips and rosy checks!
Your angelic face I regard
As the face of a saint … Bernard!
Won't you make tonight
My greatest thrill
Since the day I got disbarred?

Natasha—
I'm enamoured of you alone!
Natasha—
How I worship the ground you own!
And provided the rumours about your wealth are
true,
Natasha, I love you.

They tango

>(*Speaking*) You know, Snookums, you and I could make beautiful music together. After all you *are* shaped like a piano. Ah, I can see us now — silently stealing into our little honeymoon cottage. Just you, me, and the Russian army.

Mrs Pavlenko The Russian army?

Samovar Well, SOMEBODY's gotta carry you over the threshold.

They dance up stage and Gino suddenly emerges from behind the piano and joins them as they dance downstage. When they turn up stage, a large marathon dance number "17" is revealed on Gino's back. They continue to dance. Mrs Pavlenko realizes with annoyance that Gino has joined them. Gino gives her his leg. Mrs Pavlenko pushes it away—"Don't do that!" Samovar picks up a flower and gives it to Mrs Pavlenko. Gino grabs the stem above her hand, she grabs it above his hand with her other hand; they proceed up the stem to the flower, which Gino bites off and eats. Mrs Pavlenko tosses away the stem as the song continues

>Oh… Oh…
>Natasha—
>How I'm longing to pat that fat
>Natasha—
>Would you mind if I called you Nat?
>You've unsettled my status quo
>For you've got me all aglow
>With your beauty and money
>And breeding and money
>And sweetness and money
>And dough!

During the following, Gino fetches the stool from the desk

>Natasha—
>You're straight out of a storybook—
>I'll basha if you marry some other crook!
>Yes I'm longing to lope down the aisle with
>You know who-oo!
>For despite your pronounced moustacha,
>Natasha, I love you… (*Speaking*) Oy vey!

They end with a flourish, twirling Mrs Pavlenko on the stool. Samovar throws himself across her lap. They pose for a moment. Then, to music, Samovar and

Mrs Pavlenko dance over to the chaise longue and sit together. Gino replaces the stool and goes to collapse, exhausted, in a chair above Carlo

(*Speaking*) Well, what do you say, Muscles?

Mrs Pavlenko Oh, Serge, what can I say, but yes! Yes! Yes! (*She pulls him to her*) Isn't it strange the way we were thrown together?

Samovar It certainly is strange the way *you* were thrown together!

They sit together on the chaise longue

> *Constantine enters L, as Nina enters R; she is followed almost immediately by Sascha and Masha*

Constantine Nina, if you'd only let me explain!

Nina (*rushing to him*) Darling, you don't have to, I've read your play. Oh what a fool I've been, a blind headstrong fool!

Constantine Oh, Nina!

Nina Oh, Constantine!

Constantine & Nina (*singing, unaccompanied*) Again united...

Carlo slams the keyboard lid shut and folds his arms determinedly

Samovar (*after an approving look, going over to Carlo and shaking his hand; to the audience*) Well, that seems to wind up the plot very neatly. The young lovers are happy. (*He gestures to Mrs Pavlenko*) She's happy, I'm happy. (*He gestures to Gino and Carlo*) They're happy. (*He gestures to Masha and Sascha*) They're happy ... whoever they are. In fact, the only one who *isn't* happy is the author, Anton Chekhov. He wanted my part played by Basil Rath— (*he coughs*) Basil Rath— (*he coughs*) sorry, the bone got stuck in my throat. (*To the audience*) But anyway, thank you for being a lovely crowd. (*To Mrs Pavlenko*) And thank *you* for being a lovely crowd. (*To the audience*) But shucks, folks, I don't want to bore you with a lot of flattery. Instead let me bore you with a closing chorus. May I have a chord please?

Carlo opens the lid of the keyboard. Gino triumphantly produces a thick rope, tied in a noose, which he hands to Samovar. Samovar takes it resignedly and puts it around his neck

Thank yaw!

Song 23: A Night in the Ukraine (Finale)

Carlo   It looks like ev'rything turned out all right.
                      Dis-a night
                      In the Ukraine.

Gino pantomimes singing the next eight bars—with big operatic gestures, honking the notes

As Mrs Pavlenko sings the following, Samovar, Carlo and Gino all react with displeasure or boredom

Mrs Pavlenko (*slowing down the tempo*)
                         The snow was heavy, but my heart was light
                         On a night…
Samovar Tell me, is your voice trained?
Mrs Pavlenko Why yes, yes, it is.
Samovar Well, why don't you train it to roll over and play dead?
  (*Singing*)   Said Samovar
                         The lawyer!
All   He's the legal eagle who can boast
                         Quite the most
                         Limited brain
                         So hail the lawyer with the big cigar
                         No one's luckier than Samovar—
Samovar   'Cause I was born beneath a lucky czar!
All   Oh what a night in the Ukraine
                         Hey!

Gino takes out a sign with "HEY!" on it

Curtain calls

CURTAIN

THROUGH FOR FOLDING DROP

DRESSING/WAITING AREA

ESCAPES

DANCE BAR

ANKLE - STAGE
(9', 3½" above stage floor)

DRESSING/WAITING AREA

ESCAPES

"A NIGHT IN THE UKRAINE" TRACK w/BLACK VELOUR

ENTRANCE

DRESSING BOOTHS

EXIT +9'-3½ ABOVE WAGON

EXIT

EXIT +5" BELOW

REVOLVING DOORS

#1 #2 #3 #4 #5 #6

RAMP UP TO +5"

PIANO

PIANO PIVOTS ON D.S. LEG

SWIVEL STOOL

COUNTER

ENTRANCE

CURT. RIG.

OB-STRUCT'N

BENCH

BENCH

SCENE DESIGN

"A DAY IN HOLLYWOOD"

FURNITURE AND PROPERTY LIST

ACT I
A DAY IN HOLLYWOOD

THE MOVIES GET YOU THROUGH

On stage: Piano. *On upstage side*: pouch containing spectacles and pipe for **Carlo**)
Swivel stool
2 benches

Off stage: 5 slim, round, black shiny cushions that can be kneeled on. All 5 have a red star on one side. On the flip side, 3 cushions have a photograph each of a different Marx Brother, i.e. Groucho, Harpo and Chico. The remaining 2 cushions each have a gold star (**5 Ushers**, all except **Carlo**)

MR SID GRAUMAN
Cane (**ASM** or **Swing Dancer**)

FAMOUS FEET
"Charlie Chaplin" — Cane (**Nina**)
"Sonja Henie" — Ice skates (**Mrs Pavlenko**)
"Tom Mix" — Cowboy boots (**Constantin**)
"Marlene Dietrich" — Chair (**Nina**)
"Judy Garland" — Ruby slippers (**Masha**)
"Dracula" — Black cloak (**Constantin**)
"Dorothy Lamour" — Sarong, flowers round her bare ankles (**Mrs Pavlenko**)
"Al Jolson" — White gloves (**Constantin**)
"Mickey Mouse" — Yellow clogs, black tail (**Sascha**)
"Minnie Mouse" — Yellow clogs, black tail with red bow on it (**Masha**)

WHERE ELSE BUT ON THE SILVER SCREEN?
Arrow (**Samovar**)

A DAY IN HOLLYWOOD
Mop, owlish spectacles, wig with curlers (**Mrs Pavlenko**)

After A DAY IN HOLLYWOOD
Suitcase (**Masha**)

TINSELTOWN
Suitcase (**Gino**)

THE STORY BEHIND THE SONG
Clapperboard, on which are chalked the words "THE STORY BE-
HIND THE SONG", floppy cap (**Samovar**)

OVER THE RAINBOW
"Judy Garland" — Ruby Slippers, rainbow-lined cape
Step-unit, with clip-on "Yellow Brick Road"

IT ALL COMES OUT OF THE PIANO
White gloves with black markings, to suggest that the fingers are the
  black and white keys of a keyboard (when hands are palm down)
  (**Masha, Sascha, 4 Ushers**)

AIN'T WE GOT FUN
Clarinet (**Samovar**)

TOO MARVELOUS FOR WORDS
Clarinet (**Samovar**)

JAPANESE SANDMAN
Ukelele (**Constantin**)
Chopsticks (**Gino**)

ON THE GOOD SHIP LOLLIPOP (VERSION 1)
Baritone saxophone (**Mrs Pavlenko**)

ON THE GOOD SHIP LOLLIPOP (VERSION 2)
W.C. Fields hat (**Samovar**)

DOUBLE TROUBLE
Melodica (**Constantin**)
Melodica (**Samovar**)

LOUISE
Straw hat (**Samovar**)

BEYOND THE BLUE HORIZON

Set: 4 units of steps behind traveller on the Ankle-stage

THANKS FOR THE MEMORY
Off stage: White scarf, gloves (**Constantin**)
White 1930's hat, gloves (**Nina**)

DOIN' THE PRODUCTION CODE
White gloves, gold tap shoes (**Ushers**)

A NIGHT IN THE UKRAINE
Harpo's legs (**Sascha** and **Masha**)
"Marlene Dietrich"* — White top hat, lit cigarette in holder, chair
   (**Gino**)
*Alternatively: "Katharine Hepburn" — Wide-brimmed floppy hat,
   with ribbon

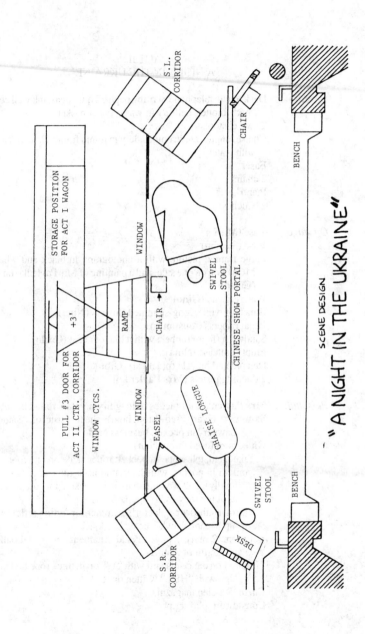

SCENE DESIGN
"A NIGHT IN THE UKRAINE"

ACT II
A NIGHT IN THE UKRAINE

On stage: Desk. *On it*: telephone, writing paper, 2 quill pens, ink well containing "ink", blotter, bell. *By it*: waste-paper basket
2 swivel stools
Chaise longue. *On it*: embroidery in round frame. *Behind it*: container with water
Easel
2 chairs
Piano
2 benches

Off stage: Vase (**Masha**)
Vase (**Sascha**)
Large framed picture with a photograph in black and white of the MGM lion on one side, and a painting of Mrs Pavlenko on the other (**Carlo**)
Watering can (**Gino**)
Bunch of white, long-stemmed flowers (**Nina**)
Legal papers (**Constantin**)
Sandwich (foam rubber) with a bite out of it (**Carlo**)
Empty suitcase (**Nina**)
Delapidated bicycle (practical) (**Gino**)
2 duelling pistols (**Mrs Pavlenko**)

Personal: **Mrs Pavlenko**: lorgnettes or magnifying glass round her neck
Samovar: cigar (used throughout), sheet music of "Samovar, the Lawyer" in pocket; business card
Gino: horn (used throughout)
fake hand, telescope in pocket; roller skate on one foot;
confetti in pocket, whistle around neck (unless actor can whistle loudly), doll wearing diapers in pocket, popcorn in a container as at the movies, lollipop;
carrot, stethoscope, doctor's hammer for testing reflexes;
zip-up banana, hawk's beak, blackjack;
broom, 2 buns, 2 large crystal ornaments or crystal balls, pullet, pocketful of feathers
marathon dance placard with "17" on it, thick rope tied in a noose, sign with "HEY" written on it
Carlo: Russian magazine
Constantin: playscript

LIGHTING PLOT

Property fittings required: nil

Various interior settings

ACT I A DAY IN HOLLYWOOD

To open: House lights dim, curtain lights dim, bring up full general lighting on main stage

Cue 1	Four **Ushers** march briefly into a line, C *Bring up lighting on Ankle-stage*	(Page 4)
Cue 2	Dance break on Ankle-stage *Concentrate lighting on Ankle-stage*	(Page 7)
Cue 3	**"Dracula"** lifts up **"Judy"** *Cross-fade to* **Samovar** *and* **Gino** *on benches on main stage*	(Page 7)
Cue 4	**Samovar & Gino**: "Oh ..." *Bring up lighting on Ankle-stage*	(Page 8)
Cue 5	**Samovar & Gino** (singing): "Like all those famous feet." *Fade lighting on Ankle-stage*	(Page 9)
Cue 6	**Mrs Pavlenko** exits L *Bring up lighting on Ankle-stage*	(Page 13)
Cue 7	**Gino** (singing): "To Tinseltown." *Black-out. When ready bring up full general lighting on main-stage*	(Page 15)
Cue 8	**Carlo**: "Everybody!" *Bring up lighting on Ankle-stage*	(Page 18)
Cue 9	The travellers close *Fade lighting on Ankle-stage*	(Page 19)
Cue 10	**Constantin and Gino** exit *Bring up lighting on Ankle-stage*	(Page 28)

Cue 11   **All** (singing): "Time! ..."   (Page 29)
            Black-out. When ready bring up full general lighting on
                main-stage

Cue 12   **Nina**: "Thanks ..."   (Page 30)
            Bring up moonlight effect on Ankle-stage

Cue 13   **Ginger** and **Fred** exit, R   (Page 32)
            Black-out. When ready bring up lighting on **Ushers** *grouped*
                at the piano

Cue 14   **All** (singing): "That'll rock the new decade."   (Page 36)
            Bring up lighting on the Ankle-stage

ACT II A NIGHT IN THE UKRAINE

To open: Black-out; when ready bring up full general lighting

No cues